THE CZECHS IN OKLAHOMA

by Karel D. Bicha

University of Oklahoma Press
Norman

*Oklahoma Image is a project sponsored by the
Oklahoma Department of Libraries
and the Oklahoma Library Association,
and made possible by a grant from the
National Endowment for the Humanities.*

Library of Congress Cataloging in Publication Data

Bicha, Karel D
   The Czechs in Oklahoma

   (Newcomers to a new land)
   Bibliography: p.
   1. Czech Americans—Oklahoma—History.   2. Oklahoma—
History.   I. Title.   II. Series.
F705.B67B52   976.6'004'9186   79-19734

CONTENTS

For Paul and Anne

ACKNOWLEDGMENTS

The preparation of even a small work such as this puts an author in the debt of an astonishing number of people. In order to write about the Czechs of Oklahoma it was necessary to meet many of them. I found the experience enlightening. I inconvenienced many of them, but they offered me extraordinary hospitality. By design most of the Czech Oklahomans I sought out were "old settlers." Their vigor was amazing. I could only conclude that they have found life in Oklahoma agreeable.

For assistance, information and advice I am especially grateful to Rev. John Michalicka, Mrs. Peter Rabstejnek, and Mr. Paul Stejskal of Oklahoma City, Mr. John Kouba of Banner, Mr. Frank Podest, Sr., of Sparks, Mr. Frank Sefcik and Mrs. Lizzie Jezek of Prague, Rev. Jerome Talloen, Mrs. Frank Vaverka and Mr. Albert Vculek of Bison, and Mr. B. R. Karban of Waukomis. Rev. Michalicka, Mr. Kouba and Mr. Stejskal read portions of the manuscript and offered useful advice. All of the others generously supplied information which I could not otherwise have obtained. To all of them I wish to say *dekuji vam mnohokrat.*

I am also grateful to Gordian Press of New York for permission to quote from Angie Debo's *Prairie City* and to *Chronicles of Oklahoma* and *Minnesota History* for permission to use material which appeared in those journals.

Professor H. Wayne Morgan of the University of Oklahoma, editor of this booklet series, and Dr. Kay Fagin, and Ms. Gloria Steffen of the Oklahoma Image Project, lent kind and good-humored assistance in many ways. My wife made sense out of handwriting which increasingly departs from good calligraphic standards and typed the manuscript with efficiency. Finally, my debt to Professor Douglas Hale of Oklahoma State University is greatest of all. He first interested me in the project, he renewed my resolve on critical occasions, and he supplied me with pertinent material which he had collected over the years. I am especially indebted to him for providing the statistical data and the map which appears near the conclusion of the third chapter of the booklet.

Special thanks are due Mr. Roger Pritchett of Prague, Oklahoma, and Mrs. Louis Hanska, Yukon, Oklahoma, for their assistance in locating photographs, and to the many individuals and institutions that have permitted me to use illustrations.

It was not possible to include the diacritical marks characteristic of the Czech spelling system in this work.

Marquette University   *Karel D. Bicha*

Chapter 1
THE CZECHS

In the course of an interview with an American reporter a Czech professional athlete recently observed, "I am always aware that many, many people do not even know where Czechoslovakia is."[1] This candid remark by a well-traveled tennis professional illustrates an unfortunate truth about the contemporary world. Peoples who live in small and out-of-the-way nations are seldom newsworthy in an era dominated by the great powers. To understand something of the Czechs, therefore, it is necessary to offer an introduction to the people and their historical existence. Who are the Czechs? What part of the world have they occupied historically? And, most important, why did so many of them eventually make new homes for themselves so far from their homeland? These are important questions, and they deserve detailed answers.[2] The first two chapters of this booklet will be concerned with these questions.

The Czechs are a small nation, Slavic in language and culture, but influenced greatly by the German culture with which they have lived in close proximity for more than a thousand years. Collectively speaking, they have lived precariously since the fifth century of the Christian era in the center of Europe. They have existed both as an independent nation and as one constituent of the large, multinational empire of the Austrian Habsburgs. Their homeland, now the western half of Czechoslovakia, consists of two distinct geographical regions called Bohemia and Moravia. Bohemia, the larger and westernmost of the two regions, derived its name from the Boii, a Celtic people who inhabited the region before the arrival of the Slavic tribes who eventually became the Czechs. Moravia, a smaller region which lies east of Bohemia, acquired its name from the Morava, the major river of the region. Together, Bohemia and Moravia are slightly larger than the state of Maine.

The Czechs in Oklahoma

In the nineteenth century it was common for the Czechs, especially those who emigrated to America, to refer to themselves as Bohemians or Moravians. Often this produced confusion among native Americans who were faced with the problem of sorting out the elements of an increasingly diverse population. The problem, however, is easily resolvable. "Bohemian" and "Moravian" are geographical terms; "Czech" is a linguistic and cultural term. Czech is the preferable term, and it will be used whenever possible in the pages which follow.

Unfortunately, the word "Czech" itself is somewhat confusing. Czech is actually the Polish spelling of the word *Cech,* and the adoption of this variant in English-language writing results from the fact that the diacritical marks which are common in the Czech system of writing are not reproducible in English-language printing facilities. *Cech* is a proper noun, the name of a legendary Slavic chieftain who, allegedly, stood on a hilltop north of the present-day city of Prague, the capital and principal urban center of Czechoslovakia, and claimed the territory for his people. This event, probably fictitious, occurred before the Slavic peoples became differentiated on the basis of individual languages. Eventually Czech evolved as a distinctive western Slavic language, related to Polish and even more closely to Slovak, the language of the other large nationality group in modern Czechoslovakia. It is also related, though more distantly, to Ukrainian, Russian, Bulgarian, and Serbo-Croatian.

The Czech lands have been of fundamental importance in the complicated history of central Europe. Otto von Bismarck, the dominant personality in the creation of a unified Germany, once alleged that whoever controlled Bohemia controlled Europe. Bismarck's reference was to the strategic geographical position of Bohemia, not to the importance of Bohemia's population or resources. Bohemia is a fortress, a plain surrounded on three sides by forested mountains, and it is the geographical key to the broad plains of the Danube basin to the east, the Balkans to the south, and the Germanies to the north and west. Bohemia's location explains much of its history, and for hundreds of years rival seekers after power in Europe contested for control of this strategic and fertile land.

Though Slavic tribes settled in Bohemia and Moravia in the fifth century, their subsequent political and cultural development was not particularly rapid. Historians use such terms as Samo's state and Greater Moravian Empire to describe early efforts to form a nation, but the administrative machinery associated with these creations was rudimentary. In the ninth century, however, the principal Czech chieftains embraced Christianity, first in its Byzantine and later in its Latin or Roman Catholic form. By the tenth century power among the Czechs had become centered in Bohemia, and the Czechs had already formed a basic cultural attachment to western Europe. This meant, in particular, that the Czechs had begun to interact with the vital German culture of the surrounding regions. By the time of the noted Prince Vaclav, whose pacific policy toward the Germans provoked his brother and rival to murder him in 929, these facts of Czech life were already evident. Vaclav, of course, became a legendary character after his death—the Good King Wenceslaus of the English Christmas carol—and his statue is prominent in the main square of Prague.

Eventually the Czechs formed a recognizable kingdom whose fortunes depended upon the capabilities of a royal family known as the Premyslids. This family produced strong and ambitious rulers, but the relationships among its members were rarely amicable. Some Czech kings died prematurely and from other than natural causes. To protect and strengthen the Bohemian kingdom the Premyslid kings adopted a policy of attracting German settlers to live in Bohemia and Moravia, especially on the borders of the kingdom. With generous concessions from the Czech kings, moreover, the Germans became the town builders and the commercially-oriented town dwellers of Bohemia and Moravia. Germans eventually comprised about 30 percent of the population, and as a result of their own policy the Czechs laid the basis for the most enduring problem in their history— Czech-German cultural and economic conflict.

The last Premyslid ruler of Bohemia died in 1306, and from that date until the creation of modern Czechoslovakia in the last days of World War I a native Czech governed the affairs of the people for only a thirteen-year period in the fifteenth century. In the Bohemian kingdom the nobility elected the monarchs, and the nobles offered the crown to a member of the royal family of Luxembourg. With the accession of the Luxembourgers, Bohemia entered the golden age of its history. The second monarch in the Luxembourg line, Charles IV, was also emperor of that peculiar collection of principalities, mostly German, called the Holy Roman Empire. Charles made Prague the imperial center, lavishly endowed the city with public improvements, attracted writers and painters, and, directly and indirectly, inspired

3

many of the architectural masterpieces which still grace the city. Among the most important monuments of his thirty-two-year reign (1346-1378) were the creation of the Charles University, the oldest university in central Europe, and the construction of the Charles Bridge across the Vltava (Moldau) River. After 600 years this bridge is still is use. A local legend holds that its durability is the result of a decision to mix eggs with the mortar, thus relieving a difficult problem of oversupply in the local produce markets.

National success and prestige, of course, always produce problems of considerable magnitude, and the experience of Bohemia during its great days was no exception. From the earliest settlement of Slavic people in Bohemia and Moravia, a single word well expresses the role which they played. The word is *salient*. Czechs were a salient or wedge people, a Slavic intrusion into the area of German culture, a Slavic island in a German sea. While the implications of physical and cultural salience were considerable, by the end of the fourteenth century the Czechs began to fulfill another salient function, this time in the realm of religion. In the end they were able to drive the first successful wedge of dissent into the structure of medi-

The Czech Lands

eval Catholicism and to establish the first Protestant nation-state in Europe.

As Bohemia became wealthy and powerful, the Roman Catholic church within its borders became privileged, potent, and corrupt. These were troubled times for the church and especially for the papacy, but in Bohemia the material success of the Church was remarkable. As an institution, the Catholic church came into possession of nearly half of the developed land in the nation, and the worldliness of its leadership represented a thorough departure from its ideals. Reform of this state of affairs occurred in Bohemia a full century before the appearance of Martin Luther, John Calvin, and the other architects of the Protestant Reformation. The Czech reform came largely from within the clergy. Though there were many capable reformers at work by the end of the fourteenth century, the movement in Bohemia eventually centered in the heroic figure of John Hus, a young priest who preached at Bethlehem Chapel in Prague and actually represented the moderate faction among the reformers.

In 1415 Hus, already excommunicated, died at the stake after condemnation by the churchmen at the Council of Constance. Much of Bohemia then revolted against Rome, and for the next fifteen years the kingdom underwent the horrors of a period known as the Hussite Wars. The demands of the reformers, as expressed in a 1419 document called the "Four Articles of Prague," included the elimination of much of the institutional wealth of the Church, the public punishment of "sin," the free preaching of the gospel in the Czech language, and the administration of the Eucharist in "both kinds," that is, the giving of both the host and the chalice wine to the laity. In order to secure these demands, which the papacy refused to concede, the Czech reformers had to confront the Vatican, the Holy Roman Empire, and their own internal divisiveness.

The reformers were not of a single mind, and many Czechs also retained their allegiance to Rome. Two principal Protestant bodies crystallized out of the reform movement. One group, usually called Utraquists or Calixtines because of their emphasis on the chalice for the laity, emerged dominant and in 1434 secured a grudging papal acceptance for their precepts. The second body of reformers, called Taborites, operated from the fortress town of Tabor in southern Bohemia. Their principles were more radical, much closer to those of the Protestant reformers of the sixteenth century. Until the Utraquists crushed the Taborites in 1434 and became *the* national church, it was the evangelical, sometimes fanatic, Taborites who provided

5

the military strength necessary to preserve the nation in the face of attacks by the German Catholic forces of the Holy Roman Empire. For a time the Taborite armies of the one-eyed general Jan Zizka, using peasant troops and fortified battle wagons, took the reform cause out of Bohemia itself and wrought havoc in other parts of central Europe.

Therefore, from the fifteenth century until the early seventeenth century, Bohemia-Moravia was technically a Protestant state. It had a sizable Catholic minority, and the Utraquists were not very protestant Protestants. Commitment to the cause of reform wavered, and the cosmopolitanism of the age of Charles IV gave way to national provincialism. In 1526 the Czech nobles offered the crown to the strongly Catholic Austrian Habsburgs, and members of this famous and prolific family became the "permanent" royal family of Bohemia and Moravia. Protestantism weakened, and, in 1618, when the Czech nobility finally recognized how far their position had deteriorated, their attempt to transfer the crown to a Protestant provoked the famous Thirty Years' War. In 1620, in one of the first encounters of the war, the Czech Protestants engaged the Habsburg-led armies at a place near Prague called *Bila Hora* or White Mountain. Here they lost a battle and a nation, but they had really conceded their independence long before.

Thus, after 1620, the Czech lands became a part of the Habsburg Empire and remained a part of it for nearly 300 years. The Catholic Counter Reformation, dominated by the Jesuit order, came to Bohemia, and by 1700 Protestantism existed in the former nation only in secret enclaves. Execution or exile was the fate of the native Czech nobility, and the nobility became foreign, mostly German, in nationality. That the Czechs lost a native aristocracy in the seventeenth century is a fact of enormous significance for the future development of the people. The Czech language ceased to be a literary vehicle, and German replaced it as the language of administration, culture, and education. For nearly three hundred years the Czechs were to exist as a minority people in a land in which they were a numerical majority.

Czech historians often call the years from the mid-seventeenth to the early nineteenth centuries "the darkness." By the early nineteenth century, however, the Czechs commenced a remarkable national revival—a revival of language, culture, and national awareness. They created institutions—museums, literary societies, theaters, even political factions—and they slowly won cultural, educational, and political concessions from the reluctant Habsburgs. The prime movers in the national revival were commoners, for the nobility, non-Czech in any case, was mostly unsympathetic. The National Theater in Prague, completed in 1881 and paid for by the contributions of thousands of little people, bears an inscription which nicely captures the spirit of the reborn self-awareness of the Czechs—*Narod Sobe* ("The Nation to Itself").

Other significant changes in Czech life occurred as a result of important developments in which the Czechs played only a small part. The Revolutions of 1848, for example, spread across Europe and greatly affected the future of the people. One result of the revolutions of that year in the Habsburg lands was the final abolition of serfdom, and with this abolition came the right of the peasants to leave the land to which they had been bound and to seek their fortunes elsewhere. In addition, the Habsburgs gradually permitted a rehabilitation of the Czech language, which for two centuries had been used only by peasants, housemaids, cooks, farmhands, and domestic servants. And the results of 1848 also produced political exiles.[3]

Bohemia and Moravia were rich in resources, and after 1848 industrial development in these Habsburg provinces proceeded rapidly. This, of course, resulted in a large-scale rural to urban movement of population. A considerable consolidation and commercialization also occurred in agriculture, destabilizing peasant culture and the lives of people in the numerous peasant villages. Czechs left the countryside in large numbers, settling in Prague, smaller Czech industrial centers, Vienna—and America. Population growth was remarkable—from four to seven millions—and by 1914, 70 percent of Habsburg industrial capacity was in the Czech lands. And in the two generations following 1848 the development of the Czech lands and the development of the United States became closely entwined.

It is important to realize that the historical experience of the Czechs in Bohemia and Moravia conditioned the behavior of the Czech immigrants in America. Three aspects of Czech history are of particular importance in this regard. In the first place, the Czechs existed for a long and critical period of time with no native aristocracy and in the position of a subject people. As a consequence Czech society reflected marked democratic values. Second, the Czechs were historically a Protestant people who were involuntarily recatholicized. As a consequence of this fact religious life among Czech immigrants in America quickly displayed peculiar characteristics. Much of the distinctiveness of the Czechs as an immigrant group is the result of these two aspects of their European experience. Third, as a result of the "national revival" which entered its most intense phase during the years in which Czechs emigrated in large numbers to the United States, the immigrants from Bohemia and Moravia arrived in America with a heightened consciousness of their distinctive culture and a commitment to its preservation.

Chapter 2

THE CZECHS IN AMERICA

The Revolutions of 1848 had far-reaching implications for the Habsburg Empire. One of the most significant effects was the imperial decree abolishing the last vestiges of serfdom. In the Czech lands, and elsewhere in the Habsburg domain, peasants were at last freed from the obligations which bound them to the land and to their masters. The masters, of course, secured compensation from departing peasants. Czech peasants were the first Habsburg subjects to use their newly won freedom, and in the two generations after 1848, increasing numbers of them sought new homes in the United States. Others emigrated to Vienna or found employment in the growing industrial centers of Bohemia and Moravia. Reorganization of landholding by the increasingly commercially conscious landlords further accelerated the departure of Czech peasants from the countryside.[1]

The great majority of Czechs who emigrated to the United States between 1848 and 1914, and especially those who migrated before the 1890s, shared a common peasant background. They were former serfs or children of former serfs. As a system, serfdom evolved late in central and eastern Europe and persisted long after it had disappeared in western Europe. Serfdom, of course, meant that peasants worked on the land of a particular master under a system of law and custom which effectively bound peasant families to the land in perpetuity. Masters exercised legal jurisdiction over their peasants, and though peasants occupied a recognized social position far from the bottom of society, their ties to the masters were degrading and socially incapacitating. Hence the word "peasant" is a pejorative. It evokes an image of a dull, slow-witted, superstitious, quarrelsome, and uneducated person. Like most stereotypes, the image of the peasant contains both truth and falsehood.[2]

Some 35 million Europeans emigrated to the United States between 1820 and 1930, and the vast majority of them chose the years between 1848 and 1914 to make the transition. Approximately 300,000 of these people were Czechs. The Czechs, therefore, comprised a relatively small immigrant group. And the migrants of 1848 were not the first Czechs to seek American homes, nor were the migrants of 1914 the last of their countrymen to seek refuge in the New World. Moreover, the Czech emigration was not a random movement in either a personal or a regional sense. It represented the relocation of both individual and extended families who made collective decisions to escape a deteriorating way of life in the peasant villages of Bohemia and Moravia. It did not involve all of the Czech lands. Most of the migrants before 1900 came from southern Bohemia and eastern Moravia, two densely populated regions of poor soil and productivity.[3]

Although the bulk of the migrants were peasant farmers, many of them had also doubled as craftsmen and artisans in their villages. Among the immigrants in America, therefore, were many coopers, saddlers, harnessmakers, tinsmiths, carpenters, masons, tailors, and shoemakers. Journalists, intellectuals, and political rebels of urban origins also appeared among the early settlers in America. By 1900 the sources of Czech immigration had changed radically. After that date the usual migrants were skilled factory workers seeking improved conditions of labor in American industry. The new industrial elite in the Czech lands had begun to complain of labor shortages by 1910.[4] In general the Czech immigrants reflected a high level of skills, and only 40 percent of them relocated in America as farmers.

Emigration, moreover, was an attractive alternative primarily to the middle level of the Czech peasantry. Well-established peasants with larger holdings adapted well to commercial agriculture, while cottagers and agricultural day laborers lacked the means or the disposition to make such a radical transformation in their lives. The world departed by the immigrants, however, was the tiny one of the peasant village, for Czech peasants uniformly lived in villages and walked to their little strips of farmland each morning. And the villages themselves were uniform—100 to 150 brick or stone houses on a single dusty lane, plastered, whitewashed, and roofed with red tile. One entered each house through a large gate and proceeded by a passageway to two entrances, one leading to living quarters, the other to the stable. The inhabitants, human and animal, thus lived under a single roof. Living quarters consisted of rooms, from one to four in number, heated by a single kitchen stove. Floors were of wood, swept clean daily. Aside from these nondescript cottages, each village had a green, which also served as a marketplace, and some larger structures — a school, a church, and a *hospoda,* i.e., a tavern or public house. A brook bisected each village, and here the women gathered to wash and gossip while children tended the inevitable flocks of arrogant geese. A more panoramic view of the village environs would yield common forest and pasture land and innumerable strips of tilled soil. Both men and women worked in the fields, and the holdings of each family were often widely separated from each other.[5] The Czech immigrant who ultimately located in a bustling city in mid-America obviously underwent a wrenching personal transformation. But the same was true of the thousands of Czechs who secured farmland in the Middle West or Southwest. In America the farm houses were isolated structures, and the outbuildings were not part of the family home. The horizon normally yielded no sights except fields and sky. There were no villages near at hand, no green and commons, no instant sociability, no church or school close by, no brook, and, as often as not, no geese. The Czech peasant who became an American farmer gained something in the trade. He obtained more land, possibly even better land. But he also lost something, and his wife and children lost even more than he.

In the Czech village everyone had his or her place in a structured society, but in America a man or woman had only his or her personal resources upon which to depend. The elaborate mutual assistance features of village life were impossible to duplicate in America, and the immigrant exchanged a corporate existence for an individual one. In a social sense emigration exacted a fearful toll, and in an immigrant letter of the 1850s a Czech farmer in Minnesota Territory recognized this sad truth when he wrote: "There is much truth in the saying that whoever emigrates to America makes his lot worse, for he sacrifices himself that his descendants may fare better. For these most of all, as you know, we immigrated here."[6]

Nevertheless, the Czechs came to America, and, with rare exceptions, they remained and adjusted. The emigration was, in fact, a part of the national revival of the people, a by-product of economic change and what American social scientists later called the "revolution of rising expectations." It was a gradual, sustained movement of families whose members embarked for America from Bremen, Hamburg, or Le Havre on the usual immigrant ships, entered the United States through New York, Baltimore, New Orleans, or Galveston, and proceeded to inland destinations. The numbers in any given year were never large, and the total Czech emigration for the 1848–1914 period was not much larger than the German-speaking emigration of the single year 1882 — a banner year for the Germans. Only in the seven years before 1914 did the number of Czech immigrants exceed 10,000 persons. The thirteenth census of the United States, conducted in 1910, estimated the number of Czechs in America to be 228,738. With the addition of their American-born children, estimated to be 310,654, the census officials arrived at a figure of 539,392 "first and second generation foreigners" of Czech extraction resident in the country.[7]

Czech immigrants and Americans of Czech extraction were only a small fraction of the American population. However, they exhibited distinctive regional preferences and concentration occurred to an appreciable extent. With the exceptions of a large community in New York City and a smaller one in Baltimore, the Czechs located in the middle western states, from Ohio to the Dakotas, Nebraska, and Kansas, and in the Southwest, in Texas and Oklahoma. In essence the timing of the emigration from Bohemia and Moravia coincided with the rapid development of mid-America, and the locational preferences of the Czechs reflected this basic fact. And, with the exception of the settlements in the Dakotas, Nebraska, Kansas, and Oklahoma, the geographical contours of Czech America were already apparent by the late 1850s.

Though the great majority of Czech immigrants who arrived before 1900 were persons of peasant background, only about 40 percent of Czech-Americans settled on farms. This is a considerably higher percentage than was customary for Slavic immigrants in general. It resulted from the fact that Czechs emigrated earlier than other Slavic peoples while America still had arable land to offer. The Czechs loved the land, and a larger percentage of the second generation lived on farms than did the first generation. A majority of Czechs, immigrants and second generation, pursued their livelihoods in the rapidly growing cities of mid-America.

The chronology of Czech settlement in the United States is easy to sketch.[8] The first urban colony developed in St. Louis, and the first farm settlements appeared in Wisconsin along the shore of Lake Michigan from Racine to Kewaunee. Both of these developments occurred in the early 1850s. Shortly thereafter Moravian Czechs established the first of many communities in east central Texas, and in the mid-1850s Czech farmers established themselves in eastern Iowa and in Minnesota Territory both south and west of St. Paul. The beginnings of the Czech communities in Baltimore, New York, and Cleveland also date from the early and middle 1850s. In the early 1860s the first Czechs appeared in Chicago, and the beginnings of the numerous settlements in eastern Nebraska date from the late 1860s. Czechs settled in central Kansas in the mid-1870s in an organized colonizing venture, and in the late 1870s other Czechs settled in a number of places in eastern Dakota Territory. And after 1889 Czech farmers began to settle on the recently opened lands of Oklahoma Territory.

A middle-American orientation in Czech settlement preferences was obvious. Equally obvious was the inclination of Czechs to settle close to Germans, for despite the hostility which characterized their relations in the Czech lands, most Czechs also spoke German and owed much to German influences. The original settlements also established the outlines of Czech America, but within those outlines the relative importance of the particular settlements changed considerably. Nevertheless, where Czechs settled in appreciable numbers by 1890, their descendants are still resident. Where Czechs did not locate by that date, there are few persons of Czech ancestry.

While the first urban colony appeared in St. Louis, and while Racine, Wisconsin, enjoyed the reputation of the "Czech Bethlehem," neither St. Louis nor Wisconsin remained long at the forefront of Czech America.[9] Three large urban colonies, New York, Cleveland, and Chicago, eventually eclipsed St. Louis as major Czech centers. Wisconsin yielded its position as the preeminent Czech agricultural state to Nebraska and Texas. Omaha became a more important center of Czech life than St. Louis, and some early centers of concentration such as Baltimore and Milwaukee declined in importance. The Czech populations of Wisconsin, Minnesota, Iowa, and Kansas stabilized in size by 1890, while the settlements in Nebraska and Texas continued to grow slowly.

Regardless of location, Czech farmers in the United States practiced diversified and self-sufficient agriculture. Czech urban dwellers, except for the residents of Chicago, became increasingly specialized in their occupations. Cigar-making and the manufacture of pearl buttons predominated among the Czechs of New York, while Cleveland Czechs became skilled factory operatives. By the mid-1880s, however, Chicago emerged as the center of Czech-American life, and by 1910 more people of Czech extraction lived in Chicago than in any city in the world except Prague. Nearly a fourth of all Czech

Americans resided in the Chicago area, and the Czech community was so diverse that it constituted a city within the city. Nearly all ordinary goods, services, and recreational opportunities were available within a Czech-speaking environment.

Czech immigration on a large scale ended with World War I. With the cementing of a Czech-Slovak partnership in 1918, the Czechs again became part of an independent nation-state. Social and cultural reasons for emigration became superfluous. There was some emigration to the United States in the 1920s and 1930s, but after 1924 the imposition of the quota system insured that the numbers would be small. Moreover, the creation of Czechoslovakia also entailed the creation of a new nationality—Czechoslovak. American immigration authorities took due note of this in 1921. After that date it is impossible to discern from official data if immigrants were Czechs, Slovaks, or others who held Czechoslovak citizenship. There was some relaxation of the quota to accommodate refugees from the Nazi occupation of 1938, the Communist coup of 1948, and the Soviet invasion of 1968, but the refugee immigrants who entered the United States in the wake of these national disasters were largely government officials, writers, and intellectuals, an elite with few if any ties to their predecessors. They were numerically few, and averaged less than 1,000 a year for the period 1946–1975.[10] The common folk, the raw material of Czech-American life, had arrived before 1914.

Chapter 3

CZECH SETTLEMENT IN OKLAHOMA

There were some fast Bohemians
And mules one lovely pair
They beat the mounted squadron
Of course they did it fair.[1]

In opening the Unassigned Lands to agricultural settlement in a piecemeal fashion after 1889, the federal authorities deliberately created the last agricultural frontier in the continental United States. Oklahoma was also the last place in America to which Czech immigrants and Czech Americans migrated in search of farmland. Czechs participated in the settlement of Oklahoma from the outset, and used all of the extraordinary techniques which made Oklahoma pioneers so notable in American folklore. Like Oklahoma settlers in general, the Czechs who found their way to the new territory fell into two distinct categories—the Sooners and the slower folk. The Sooners were few in numbers, the slower folk were much more prominent.

April 22, 1889, is one of the famous dates in the annals of the American frontier. The "run" into the Unassigned Lands and the instant creation of Guthrie and Oklahoma City represented the fruits of a generation of pressure to open the Indian Territory and the payoff for the sustained labors of the so-called boomers. That the land rush produced both a carnival-like atmosphere and an instant mythology often obscures a basic truth. For many people with a deep commitment to the land, Oklahoma was the last chance. Failure to secure a claim in the new Territory might mean the end of farming as a way of life. These circumstances strained the patience of a very impatient people.[2]

Oklahoma did not acquire its nickname of "Sooner State" just because some local wit invented it. Its settlers earned it. Federal officials estimated that as many as a third of those who entered the Territory in the "run" of 1889 disregarded the official timetable in order to secure a share of Oklahoma's land.[3] Among the Sooners were at least twenty-five Czechs, previously resident in Nebraska, led by a determined and strange man named Anton Caha. The story of the Czechs in Oklahoma begins with this peculiar captain, his followers, and his celebrated pair of mules.

Anton Caha was a Moravian, born in the village of Klanchov either in 1852 or 1856. His father was a professional soldier, commander of the Austrian army regiment quartered at Brno, the principal city of Moravia. He was also a professional troublemaker, and for revolutionary activity against the Habsburgs he forfeited both his property and his life. His widow soon remarried, and with her new husband and two sons, Anton and Josef, emigrated to the United States in the 1860s. She settled eventually in a growing Czech colony

Anton Caha. From *Portrait and Biographical Record of Oklahoma.* Courtesy of the Western History Collections, University of Oklahoma.

16

in Colfax County, Nebraska. Here Anton Caha grew to manhood, married, and established a creamery which prospered for many years. In the Second Sioux War, the 1876 conflict which Americans associate with Sitting Bull, George Custer and the Little Big Horn, Caha raised a militia company, secured the title of captain, and in one skirmish with the Indians sustained a painful wound—ironically, in the knee. Eventually, however, Caha's business began to decline. After some severe financial reverses, he began to seek alternative areas for his activities. The future, he judged, was in Oklahoma, and Caha organized an expedition to the greener pastures.[4]

Like a true captain, Caha formed a company of Nebraska Czechs, and the company, well organized and well provisioned, traveled by rail from Omaha to Purcell, Oklahoma. From Purcell the Caha company moved heavy wagons to a place on the South Canadian River near the site of Tuttle. Caha's own wagon was mule drawn. The Caha company then awaited the opening of the Unassigned Lands at high noon, April 22, 1889. While encamped, the personnel of the Caha expedition surrendered to a primal temptation—greed. And greed born of impatience prompted a costly change of plans. Anticipating the opening by a few hours, Caha and his associates forded the river and moved their wagons thirteen miles to locations near the confluence of Mustang Creek and the North Canadian River, the area now between Yukon and Oklahoma City. Fifteen minutes after the legal opening, land seekers traveling on fast horses noticed Caha digging postholes on his "claim." His wagon had been unloaded, and his mules, tethered and apparently well rested, calmly grazed on the prairie grass.[5]

The claims of Caha, his brother Josef, and the other members of his company were challenged. This was not peculiar to these beleaguered Czechs, for hundreds of claims were contested in the courts. But the mules added a unique dimension to Caha's predicament. In the federal court case involving his claim, Caha responded to the question of how he succeeded in covering thirteen miles in fifteen minutes in a wagon pulled by a pair of mules. He attributed the feat to the swiftness of his mules. His explanation was unsophisticated, unconvincing, and untrue. The jury convicted him of perjury, and his compatriots from Nebraska fared no better in five other court cases. They forfeited their claims, and most of them served brief terms in jail. Caha's sentence was more severe. He spent two years in the federal prison at Leavenworth, Kansas, and returned to Oklahoma upon his release. In all of the cases the government attorneys worked

17

on the assumption that if one Bohemian was guilty all were guilty.[6]

Like his father, Anton Caha had a propensity for trouble. Unlike his father, however, Caha rehabilitated himself. His wife died while he was in prison, but she had had the foresight to buy a quarter section of land near Keokuk Falls, Pottawatomie County. Though she was dead and his children scattered, Caha was not without resources. He settled on the homestead, remarried, sired more children, and built a sawmill and cotton gin. He also served in the Spanish-American War. In the course of a thirty-two-year residence in the Keokuk Falls area, which ended with his death in 1927, this crusty and strong-willed immigrant reestablished his reputation as a solid citizen.[7] In 1901, only six years after his release from prison, his biography appeared in the *Portrait and Biographical Record of Oklahoma.* The author found it prudent to omit the embarrassing details of Caha's past, observing only that, "upon locating upon a contested claim, he lost the remainder of a hard-earned competency."[8] While this facile explanation was in no way untrue, it neatly avoided the reality of Caha's past activities.

Thus Czech settlement in Oklahoma began with a group whose actions made them federal criminals. But the Sooners were few in number, and the more ordinary activities of the slower folk were of greater importance. The Czechs who came to Oklahoma in the run of 1889 or in subsequent runs, or who secured land by sale or lottery, were like the members of the Caha party. They came primarily from Nebraska, with smaller groups from Kansas, Iowa, and Texas also in evidence. They had spent many years in America, and the majority were probably American born. Many of the Nebraska Czechs had earlier lived in Wisconsin, and many of the settlers from Kansas had roots in Chicago.[9] Hence the migration of Czechs to Oklahoma was a secondary migration at best. This was not unusual, for the foreign-born population of the United States and the first generation of Americans born of foreign parentage were as mobile as the old native stock and probably more so. This is a little-realized fact of American life. The popular idea of immigrants and their descendants clinging to tightly knit farm communities or to queer, cozy "foreign quarters" in American cities and perpetuating themselves in these locations for generations has little basis in reality. Particularly in Oklahoma the Czech settlers were not "greenhorns," to use an expression for new immigrants common in the late nineteenth century. They created ethnic enclaves, not immigrant colonies.

The first principal Czech settlement in Oklahoma was in the area the Caha party itself had chosen, immediately west of Oklahoma City, especially the Yukon, Mustang, and El Reno townships of Canadian County. Here, in 1889 or shortly thereafter, a large number of Czechs settled on the land or secured employment as machinists in the repair shop of the Rock Island Railroad. Some of them lived for a time in dugouts or sod houses. Their family names were distinctive—Kroutil, Michalicka, Dobry, Kouba, Pachta, Svoboda, Rabstejnek, Stejkovsky, Pribyl, Stejskal, Kaspar, Divis, Smrchka, Zidek, Maly, Nespor, Ruzicka, Zahradka, Funda, Berousek, Skocdopole, Kassl, Karbucky, and others. Almost simultaneously other Czech families from Nebraska, Kansas, and Iowa located in Oklahoma County, both in Oklahoma City and the townships immediately east of the city. Prominent among them were the members of families named Kunc, Kratky, Bednar, Kolar, Novotny, Kosar, Swatek, Skala, Zika, Zaloudek, Hrabe, Ryndak, Yager, Straka, Petrasek, Sochor, Sudik, Berousek, Kolarik, Krivanek, Benes, Kalivoda, Hubatka, Spacek, Pesek, Muzny, Drabek, and Maruska. With few exceptions the descendants of these early Czech settlers still inhabit Canadian and Oklahoma counties.

In the run of 1889 other Czech families settled in the portion of the Unassigned Lands which became Kingfisher County. A larger number arrived in 1890 and subsequent years and acquired "relinquishment" lands—land claims vacated by original settlers because of irregularities in the settlement procedures. Among the Kingfisher County Czech settlers the prominent family names were Cabelka, Chlouber, Jech, Jindra, Kadavy, and Nakvinda. Most of the settlers came from Caldwell, Kansas, though a few had previously lived in the Nebraska communities of Sidney and North Platte. The primary concentrations of Czechs in the county were at Kingfisher, Okarche, and Cashion. In time some of the families, especially the Jechs and Jindras, became very large and active in local affairs.[10]

In spite of the recentness of settlement in Oklahoma, one of the oldest Czech colonies has already disappeared. This was the community named Mishak, located in Boone Township, Oklahoma County. The first Czechs established themselves in the township shortly after the run of 1889, but the primary period of settlement occurred between 1900 and 1905. Named in honor of a migratory Czech, Frank Mishak, who soon left the community, the town once boasted a post office, church, school, stores, and lodges of two Czech-American fraternal societies. The local farmers specialized in dairying and vegetables, and Czech families named Genzer, Hradecny,

19

Zaloudnik, and Skoch were the backbone of the community. Mishak's decline began in the 1920s when the development of the petroleum industry induced its businessmen to relocate in Marion. But it was the needs of the federal government which really sounded the death knell of the little community. Mishak's existence inhibited the plans to expand Tinker Air Force Base, and federal authorities decreed the disappearance of the town. Its residents manifested typical Czech stubbornness, but the agents of the federal government were powerful adversaries. In a series of condemnation suits in the 1940s and 1950s the descendants of the original settlers lost their properties, and the town disappeared. Only a small cemetery marks the location of the community.[11]

The second area of Czech concentration in Oklahoma resulted from the opening of the lands of the Sac-Fox reservation in 1891. In the run of September 23, 1891, a number of Czech settlers secured homesteads in the area of Lincoln County eventually associated with the village of Prague. Other Czechs soon followed, and within a decade South Creek and Seminole townships of Lincoln County had the densest concentration of Czechs in Oklahoma Territory. The earliest Czech settlers were those named Barta, Vlasak, Suva, Bontty, Eret, Benes, Mastena, and Martinet. They came from the

Broadway Street, Prague, Oklahoma, 1902, looking north. Courtesy of Mr. Conrad Knoepfli.

Nebraska communities of Crete, Ord, and Milligan, from Munden, Kansas, or from Iowa and Wisconsin. Czechs found the area attractive, and news of its suitability spread widely in Czech-American communities. After 1900 Czechs from Texas and a number of northern settlements also migrated to Lincoln County.[12]

A third, and final, area of primary Czech concentration developed north of Oklahoma City in the counties of Garfield, Grant, and Noble. Widely scattered Czech colonies appeared in these counties primarily, but not entirely, as a result of the 1893 opening of the Cherokee Strip. The territory involved was more extensive, and the Czech colonies in the area were scattered and more deeply imbedded in the general population. But the Czech settlers came from the traditional places in the other plains states. Garfield County attracted Czechs with such names as Jandera, Maly, Zavodny, Zika, Pavlik, Pospiscil, Urban, Dolezal, Vencl, Krejci, Vacek, Zeman, Klima, Hajek, Vaverka, Novotny, and Stepanek. Grant County became the new home of settlers named Lebeda, Tluhar, Skrdla, Sladek, Cink, Jez, Bruza, Jindra, Smetana, Soucek, and Kotas, while the Peterska, Hejtmanek, Folk, Jelinek, Vitek, and Blecha families pioneered in Noble County. The countryside near such villages as Bison, Waukomis, Medford, and Perry contained Czechs in appreciable numbers by 1905.[13]

Czech settlement in Oklahoma occurred almost entirely in the territorial period. Despite the differences in time of the various runs, all of the Czech settlements except Mishak and Prague appeared on a north-south line determined by the routes of the Rock Island and Santa Fe railroads. By the time of statehood in 1907 the movement was complete, and future increases in the number of Oklahomans of Czech extraction resulted from the excess of births over deaths rather than a continued migration of people. In 1906 a Czech Oklahoman named Josef Hajek estimated that the Territory contained twenty-five Czech colonies and 2,000 families.[14] Both of these estimates were too high. The federal census of 1900 noted the number of European-born Czechs as 1,168, and this figure grew only to 1,624 in the 1910 census. In 1910 the Census Bureau for the first time provided figures for "total foreign stock," that is, immigrants plus their American-born children. The Oklahoma figure was 5,633 for the Czechs.[15] Hence 1910 was probably the numerical high point for the state's Czech population, for, by Census Bureau designation, foreignness and ethnic allegiance disappear with the third generation.

The Czechs were not, and are not, a sizable part of the Oklahoma population. Nor were they a large part of its total foreign-born population. In 1910, for example, the Czechs comprised 5.8 percent of the persons of foreign stock, immigrants and first generation American-born, resident in Oklahoma. The total foreign stock represented 8 percent of the population of the state. Thus, one Oklahoman in every 300 was of Czech extraction in 1910. Nearly two-thirds of the Czechs lived in the ten north central counties, however. They achieved visibility in these counties. And, though their numbers were small, only Germans, Spanish, and Italians outnumbered them among the foreign stock of non-English language origin.[16] (Yet in 1910 Nebraska was home to 50,000 Czechs, Texas to 41,000, Minnesota to 33,000, Kansas to 12,000 and the Dakotas to nearly 10,000.) Finally, it is useful to provide a numerical summary in tabular form of the principal concentrations of Czechs in Oklahoma.

Czechs in Principal Oklahoma Counties and Townships, 1910*

Canadian County 196	*Garfield County 247*
El Reno 21	Allison 26
Mustang 36	Osborne 39
Yukon 96	Sumner 27
	Union 20
	Waukomis 15
Oklahoma County 213	Flynn 17
Boone 23	
Greeley 27	*Kingfisher County 140*
Mustang 27	Logan 23
Oklahoma City 54	Sherman 46
Grant County 157	*Noble County 187*
Fairview 33	Black Bear 36
Hickory 53	Glenrose 23
Jarvis 19	Red Rock 17
	Rock 31
	Watkins 29
Lincoln County 202	
Creek 15	*Pittsburg County 126*
South Creek 111	Bucklucksy 16
North Creek 16	Dow 80
South Seminole 45	McAlester 17

Source: Unpublished data from *Thirteenth Census of the United States, 1910.* Data provided by U.S. Bureau of the Census, Personal Service Branch.

*These data refer only to the foreign born, i.e., the immigrant generation. The counties and townships listed above domiciled 1,468 of the 1,624 Czech immigrants resident in the state in 1910. Counties with fewer than 100 Czech immigrants, and townships with fewer than 15, are not included in the table.

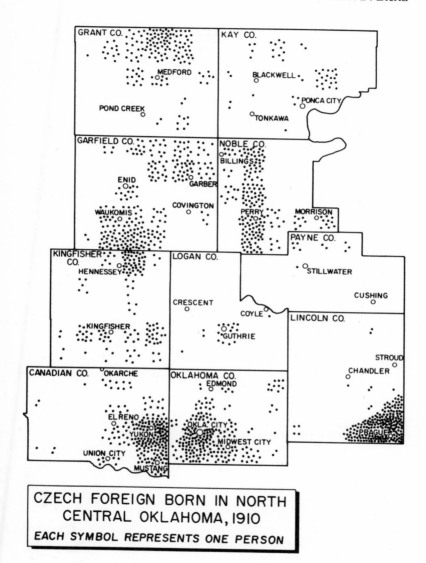

CZECH FOREIGN BORN IN NORTH
CENTRAL OKLAHOMA, 1910
EACH SYMBOL REPRESENTS ONE PERSON

Czech foreign born in North Central Oklahoma, 1910. Courtesy of the *Chronicles of Oklahoma.*

In 1910, therefore, Oklahoma's Czech population of 5,633 consisted of 1,624 immigrants and 4,009 persons born to Czech immigrant parents in the United States. Thus nearly three-fourths of Oklahoma's Czechs were the American-born offspring of immigrant parents. By way of contrast, areas of Czech concentration which received an influx of immigrants over a sustained period, e.g., Chicago, had a foreign to native-born population ratio as low as 1:1.5, a far different mix than that which characterized Oklahoma.

Finally, the Czechs who settled in Oklahoma had widely varied origins and thoroughly different backgrounds. In the 1920s, for example, Josef Bunata, a free lance Czech-American journalist and one-time socialist organizer, undertook a survey of the older Czech residents of the Prague, Oklahoma, community. He discerned no patterns worth noting. In place and date of birth in Bohemia or Moravia, previous places of residence in the United States, and occupational histories, the Czechs of Prague had little in common except their final residence and an extraordinarily large number of offspring.[17] Though Bunata neglected these factors, the Czechs in Prague, and elsewhere in Oklahoma, had other things in common—their culture, their distinctive surnames, and their accents.

The Jezek Grocery Store, Prague, Oklahoma, about 1930. Left to right, Frank Jezek, a salesman, and Charles Jezek. Courtesy of Mrs. Lizzie Jezek.

Chapter 4

THE CZECHS AND RELIGION

Immigrants in the United States, and the ethnic generations which succeeded them, possessed distinctive cultural attributes. Immigrant peoples brought to America all of the elements of their national cultures—language, cuisine, customs, beliefs, religious faiths, and behavioral peculiarities. These cultural attributes, transmitted imperfectly even to the first of the American-born generations, persist for varying periods of time and in diminishing degrees, depending upon the size, location, concentration, and peculiarities of the respective groups.

All of these observations apply to the Czechs—in Oklahoma and elsewhere in America. The Czechs, however, have been among the more persistent national groups in seeking to preserve their old-world culture. Czech immigrants came to the United States from a part of Europe in which the traditional peasant culture was deteriorating rapidly under the pressures of industrialization and agricultural commercialization. Emigration afforded the Czechs an opportunity to preserve in America cultural forms threatened in the homeland. Departure from the peasant villages of Bohemia and Moravia was a by-product of economic modernization and of the national revival. It was also a conservative response to change. Hence the American environment often produced an intense culture consciousness among the Czechs and made them, at least temporarily, more Czech than they had been at home.

Like all nationality groups, however, the Czechs went through the acculturation process required by the host society. The two cultural attributes of immigrant-ethnic groups most resistant to change are culinary preferences and religious faith. The pervasiveness of ethnic restaurants and ethnic churches in American society demonstrate this clearly. Until recently most Catholic parishes in the

United States were clearly ethnic—Irish, German, Polish, Spanish, Italian, etc. It is still accurate to associate Wisconsin and Missouri Synod Lutheranism with Americans of German extraction. The synodical bodies which represented Lutherans of Norwegian, Swedish, and Danish heritage have only recently merged to form the American Lutheran Church. The Reformed Church is Dutch-American, and the Orthodox communions are obviously ethnic. Only the "mainline" Protestant denominations and the majority of fundamentalist sects lack primary ethnic attachments. Immigrant groups transplanted their religious institutions to America with remarkable success and their descendants carefully preserved them.

The Czechs were the most noteworthy exception to this norm. In America Czech immigrants severed their allegiance to the Catholic church in large numbers. Religious conflict between Czech Catholics and their fellow countrymen who had broken with the Church was the central theme in the Czech-American experience until the 1920s. Attrition from the Catholic faith was the one element which made the Czechs a unique immigrant group. The results of religious conflict in the Czech-American community extended far beyond the matter of formal religious allegiance. Indeed, religious discord was responsible for the peculiar ways in which *all* Czech-American institutions originated and developed. Religion, therefore, is the basic key to understanding the cultural and institutional life of the Czechs in America.

The old Bohemian kingdom was the original Protestant nation in Europe, and Catholicism had been reimposed on the population after the loss of national independence. Recatholicization in the Czech lands was not a voluntary process. Nevertheless, it was successful on the surface. In each village, however, the priest fulfilled a dual role as representative of Rome and as an agent of the Habsburg, i.e., German, authority. Most peasants were probably unable to separate one role from the other. The local clergy, though commonly sympathetic to the people, found it difficult to elicit trust and understanding. Carefully concealed hostility to the institutional church was apparently widespread, especially in Bohemia, and this hostile attitude persists openly in contemporary Czechoslovakia. Under the present Communist regime only one-sixth of the nominally Catholic Czechs attend church at any time during a year. An important explanation for this laxity is that "the Church has *never* had the deep emotional following . . ."[1] which characterizes the Catholicism of nations like Poland and Ireland. The reasons, of course, are historical.

Karel D. Bicha

From the time of the earliest settlements in the United States, Czech immigrants displayed both hostility toward the Church and a willingness to break with it. Escape from the Habsburgs was apparently synonymous with escape from Rome. Official Habsburg statistics indicated that 96 percent of the population of the Czech lands professed the Catholic faith, but no more than half of the Czech immigrants in America retained their affiliation with the Church. Some observers estimated the retention rate as no more than one-third. Decatholicized Czechs did not readily affiliate with any of the Protestant denominations which competed for adherents in American society. The few Protestants among the immigrants had been Protestants in the homeland. Nearly all of the decatholicized Czechs refused to affiliate with any church and referred to themselves as "liberals," "rationalists," or, most commonly, as "freethinkers." They professed to believe in Freethought or, in Czech, *Svobodomysleni.*

Czech-American Freethought was an elusive phenomenon which defies clear definition. Freethought was not peculiar to Czech immigrants, but the Czechs embraced it on a more significant scale than any other nationality group. There were freethinking movements among all of the Slavic immigrant groups, and Freethought became prominent in the German-American community in the *Turnverein* (gymnastic) and *Freigemeinde* (free thought) societies. Among the Czechs, however, the freethinking position emerged dominant by the 1870s. But it is impossible to assess the impact of Freethought with precision. What was Freethought, and who were freethinkers? Just as significantly, how does one define a "Catholic?" There has always been great variation in the numerical estimates of the Catholic population, and Church authorities have never been particularly concerned with the calculation of precise membership data.

The definitional categories of Czech-American religious attitudes are vague, and any conclusions are at best tentative. But the freethinkers long dominated Czech-American life. They controlled the Czech-language press and the major social institutions. Freethought originated in the cultural soil of Bohemia, and the American environment merely provided the arena for its successes. Bohemia's unique religious history, the association of Catholicism with Germanization in the Czech lands, the dubious sincerity of many Czech Catholics, the breaking of the meaningful relationship between religion and the village culture which occurred with emigration, and the control over communications and opinion formation in Czech America by strategically placed freethinkers, all played a part in the decatholization of the immigrants. Moreover, there were factors in the process which were contemporary with emigration itself. In the national revival of the nineteenth century, Protestants and anticlerical liberals played the leading roles. Catholic priests active in the national revival found little appreciation for their efforts. Karel Havlicek, patriotic journalist and a famous martyr to the national cause, pronounced a harsh judgment on the Catholic clergy and opposed giving them any credit for their efforts.[2]

All of this has a direct applicability to Czech life in Oklahoma. A majority of the Czechs who settled in the new Territory were persons of freethinking disposition. Catholics were a minority among the Czech settlers and have remained a minority among Czech Oklahomans. The freethinkers were not a group with a single mind and a single purpose. Freethought was varied, and the common tendency to conclude that all Czechs who were neither formally Catholic nor formally Protestant were freethinkers is probably erroneous. The freethinkers generally fell into two categories. There was a small, militant group of agnostics and atheists, prominent in the Czech-American newspaper world and in their "free congregations." They comprised much of the leadership of Czech America and accepted a view of the origin and operation of the universe which was essentially godless. Many of these militants were former clergymen or theological students, and nearly all of them lived in the urban colonies of Czech America. A second group of free-thought advocates were simply indifferent to organized religious institutions. They were far more numerous than the militants and adopted a live-and-let-live attitude toward clergymen and churches except on those occasions when churches attempted to determine public policy.[3] For example, freethinkers in Chicago organized in 1896 to protest Bible reading in the public schools, alleging that the practice "would spoil the young hearts of our children, would deprive them of pity for humanity, good fellowship and tolerance to others, of morals, liberty and education."[4]

The primary concentrations of the "indifferent" freethinkers were in the Czech-American fraternal lodges and the *Sokol* clubs. While completely secular in attitudes, they were not necessarily atheists or agnostics. An elderly immigrant woman perhaps expressed the freethinking attitude best when she commented in 1904: "I have my God in my heart, I shall deal with Him. I do not want any priest to step between us."[5]

Few, if any, militant exponents of Freethought among the Czechs settled in Oklahoma and there were none of the "free congregations" (*svobodne obce*) typical of the militants. Hence freethinking Oklahoma Czechs were in the religiously indifferent category, and their attitudes were well formed before their arrival. Nebraska, for example, was the primary supplier of Czech settlers to Oklahoma. Many Oklahoma Czechs came from Milligan, a large Czech settlement in Fillmore County, Nebraska. Milligan was the subject of an excellent sociological study in the late 1920s. The investigator ascertained that the Czech population of this farming community was 30 percent Catholic and 70 percent "unchurched." Twenty percent of the Catholics reported their church attendance habits as "irregular." Three generations of Czechs lived in Milligan, but there was no significant variation among them in religious attitudes or habits. The unchurched Czechs regularly supported and attended the social functions of the local Catholic parish and seemed to display no hostility toward the institution. But public opinion was strongly on the side of nonmembership.[6]

Similar attitudes prevailed among the Czechs of Oklahoma. Indifference and nonmembership in churches were normal, but the only estimate of freethinker strength in Oklahoma, which specified that two-thirds of the Czechs were freethinkers, was probably too high. Nonetheless, Freethought prevailed in the lodges of the fraternal societies which soon appeared in Oklahoma, and it claimed adherents from all classes, occupations, and educational levels. Czech Catholics and native Americans aware of the extent of "infidelity" among the Czechs regarded Freethought as scandalous, but in most respects social harmony prevailed.[7]

The freethinking movement among Czech Americans had numerous positive attributes. It was very moralistic, though not fanatic or puritanical. Freethinkers advocated views on many social questions which eventually gained social respectability. They believed strongly in the separation of church and state, in civil liberties, in the scientific method of approach to social problems, and in the equality of the sexes. The emancipation of women was of particular concern, and they achieved equal status with men in the fraternal life which flourished among the freethinkers. Their absolute faith in science was perhaps naive, but they were hardly unique in the liberal community in holding such views. They were also more nationality conscious than the Catholics, and most of the attempts to preserve Czech culture in the American environment, e.g., the establishment of language schools, were the result of the efforts of freethinking groups.

Freethought was obviously individualistic, but it could not exist without organizational forms. For the most part the freethinkers operated through already existing institutions, benefit societies, fraternal lodges, and *Sokols,* which were dominated by Freethought influences. But they were insufficient, and the freethinkers expanded their functions. Just as the Church fulfilled social as well as spiritual needs and offered assistance in moments of joy and sorrow, the free-thinkers developed substitute procedures for their fellow nonbelievers. They devised rituals for the presentation of infants, marriages, and funerals, and offered assistance to the sick and the bereaved. In many ways Freethought by 1900 had become as ritualistic as the Church. And their most "permanent" monuments—institutions called in most individual cases, "Czech National Cemetery"—still dot the countryside in the areas of Czech settlement on the plains.[8]

Nevertheless, Freethought originated in old-world conditions. In America it was essentially timebound, an aspect of the transition of a nationality group to new-world conditions. Anti-Catholicism was not difficult to transmit to the children of Czech immigrants because the attitude was prevalent in American society. But anticlericalism was another matter. Americans of Czech parentage could not experience Habsburg rule, clericalism, or the political uses of the Church. Freethought was most prevalent in Czech America during the years in which Oklahoma acquired its Czech population, but it waned rapidly with the coming of World War I and the end of large-scale immigration. By the mid-1920s freethinking activity, at least in an organized context, was common only in Chicago and Cleveland. In a 1926 address to the Seventh Congress of the Freethought Union, Jaroslav E. S. Vojan, a noted Chicago publicist and Freethought spokesman, lamented the decline of the movement everywhere in America. The decline was most apparent in the plains states. Vojan described the state of Freethought in Oklahoma in one explicit sentence: "Oklahoma is silent."[9] Actually the movement breathed its last in the 1970s in Chicago, but in most of America the Freethought phenomenon had long since passed away due to a lack of issues and a lack of combatants.

Once the Freethought movement became defunct, what did Oklahoma freethinkers and their descendants do about their religious lives? They did not reaffiliate with the Catholic church to any noticeable extent, but many eventually affiliated with Protestant denominations prominent in their localities.[10]

The history of Czech Catholicism in Oklahoma, however, is much clearer. Catholics among the Czechs of Oklahoma were a minority in an area in which Catholics were an even smaller minority. Hence Czech Catholics have never been a significant element in Oklahoma's religious population. Only 2 percent of Oklahoma's people were Catholic in 1905, and only 3 percent were Catholic forty years later. Only eight Oklahoma counties contained a Catholic population as large as 5 percent in 1945, but three of these counties, Noble, Canadian, and Kingfisher, were counties of primary Czech concentration.[11] Nevertheless, Catholics have been a prominent part of Oklahoma's Czech population since the first settlements. In long run terms, Catholicism proved to be the more successful of the rival philosophies. Catholicism survived; free thought did not.

Since the early days of settlement Catholicism among the Oklahoma Czechs centered in the religious and social life of a few Czech parishes — St. Wenceslaus of Prague, founded in 1891; St. John Nepomuk of Yukon, founded in 1894; St. Martin's of Mishak, founded in 1905; and St. Joseph of Bison, founded in 1909. Two other parishes, St. Joseph of Hennessey and St. Michael of Goltry, always had a large Czech membership.[12] The history of St. Wenceslaus parish of Prague nicely illustrates the development of Czech Catholicism in Oklahoma. Originating in the year of the run into the Sac-Fox lands, the first services occurred in the homes of settlers, with visiting Benedictine priests serving as clergy. In 1899 the settlers built a rude church on land donated by a Czech farmer for cemetery purposes. Only fifteen families attended the services, but despite its small size, in 1903 the parish members provided a more adequate structure and secured the services of a Czech-speaking priest. A cyclone destroyed the second church in 1918, but rebuilding soon commenced and a third church was in use by 1921. A fourth church opened for services in 1949. In that year the parish also undertook to manage a national shrine dedicated to the Infant Jesus of Prague. Through the years the parish membership increased slowly, but Czech-speaking priests were not available after 1926. A memorial volume published in 1949, the golden anniversary of the first permanent church building, indicated that parish membership was 186, 133 of whom had Czech surnames.[13] Only a minority of Prague's residents of Czech background affiliated with the parish, however.

Catholics were always a minority among Oklahoma's Czechs. Yet they contributed some of their own to positions of importance in the Church. Thomas Havlik, one of the abbots of St. Procopius Abbey in Lisle, Illinois, the only important Czech Catholic monastery in America, came from an Oklahoma farm family. For many years this Benedictine establishment in Lisle published the most important Czech Catholic newspapers in the United States, *Narod* (*"Nation"*) and *Katolik*. Wenceslas Michalicka, the last editor of both papers, was a Czech Oklahoman. Others served in such diverse capacities as diocesan chancellors and superiors in orders of teaching and nursing Sisters.

While Catholicism endured and Freethought disappeared, the institutions built by the original freethinkers proved more popular among the Czechs than those associated with the Church. These institutions, especially fraternal societies, eventually became purely secular and lost their antichurch flavor. Yet the conflict between freethinkers and Catholics gave an unusual dimension to Czech-American life and determined the development of most of the primary Czech-American institutions.

Chapter 5

CZECH CULTURE IN OKLAHOMA: PRESS, LODGE, AND *SOKOL*

Like the members of many foreign language groups, the Czechs of Oklahoma did not immediately embrace the larger society in which they lived. In the early years and in the more isolated settlements there was often no larger society to embrace. But the Czechs, who persisted in preserving customs and folkways not always appreciated by the native settlers, tended to remain apart. There was too much cultural distance between them and their neighbors. They did not regard the larger society as congenial, and in turn many members of the larger society considered the Czechs excessively clannish. It was the influence of those gregarious creatures, children, and their educational and social needs which first brought the elders of the Czech settlements to the non-Czech population. In her remarkable account of life in Marshall, Oklahoma, Angie Debo described this process in a memorable passage. Writing about the Czech settlers of the Hennessey-Bison area west of Marshall, Miss Debo remembered the Czechs coming to trade in her beloved community, congregating on the street corners, and talking in "animated groups, filling the air with swishing consonants new to prairie ears."[1]

In the early years, however, the Czechs preferred their own company and the refuge of their own established institutions. Perhaps the severity of the religious split in the Czech community and the internal disunity fostered by religious conflict guaranteed a larger than normal measure of isolation. Disunity was a primary fact of life in Czech America. The peculiar religious configuration of the Czech community meant that the church did not fulfill the same role among the Czechs that it did among Irish or German Catholics or Norwegian or Swedish Lutherans. Given the lesser role of the church in Czech America, other institutions emerged as alternatives to the church and achieved unusual prominence. The leaders of these alternative institutions performed vital roles in the preservation of Czech self-consciousness and national identity. They were also well placed to introduce the rank-and-file inhabitants of Czech America to the values and institutions of American society. Of the numerous categories and types of Czech-American institutions, only three are pertinent to the history of the Czechs in Oklahoma—the press, the fraternal society, and *Sokol.*

Czech-Americans had a remarkable capacity to create newspapers. They had an equally remarkable capacity to destroy newspapers and to consign their publishers and journalists to oblivion. With a few exceptions, those who undertook to create a Czech-language press in America found their efforts to be a passport to impoverishment. The Czechs were a highly literate group, exceeded in literacy only by immigrants from the Scandinavian nations. Long years of struggle to keep the language alive in spite of sustained Germanization in Bohemia and Moravia produced a population with an illiteracy rate of less than 3 percent. In Bohemia and Moravia, and even more significantly in America, the newspaper became the principal medium for Czech literary expression in the nineteenth century. But publishers and readers rarely achieved a permanent rapport.[2]

From the year 1860, when the first Czech-language paper appeared in Racine, Wisconsin, to the end of 1910, some 326 Czech serial publications originated in the United States. There were eight daily newspapers, and the remaining 318 varied in frequency from semi-weekly to annual publications. By 1976 the number of newspapers and periodicals once published to serve Czech readers approximated 700, though fewer than fifty were still published in that year. There was obviously a kernel of truth in the contention of the anonymous wit who alleged that whenever two Czechs found themselves unable to resolve an argument two more newspapers saw the light of day.[3]

Czech Oklahomans lived far from the centers of Czech-American life, and their journalistic efforts clearly reflected this basic reality. There were fewer than 6,000 Czechs in 1910 in Oklahoma, and nearly three-quarters of them were American born and educated, at least partly, in an English-language environment. The potential for establishing a hardy Czech-language press in the state did not exist, but there were some interesting, and short-lived, attempts to create one. These efforts fell into two categories, a local press, and local editions of papers published in more populous Czech-American centers.

In the first category, a local press with local ownership, there were three efforts in the years from 1905 to 1910. The pioneer venture, a weekly called *Cesky Oklahoman* (*"Czech Oklahoman"*) published by the Bohemian Printing Company of Oklahoma City, first appeared in August of 1905. Dedicated to news of Czechs in Oklahoma and the South, the paper had a life-span of less than four years, suspending early in 1909. In 1907 a rival printing firm, the Czech National Publishing Society, published *Cechoslovansky Obzor* (*"Czech-Slavic Horizon"*), a weekly devoted to political, social, and agricultural matters. Publishing interests in Omaha acquired this paper before the end of 1907, and it appeared under a slightly different name until 1912. Finally, in October 1908, Sokol Havlicek in Yukon commenced a monthly newsletter of Sokol news and activities, *Havlicek*. It suspended before 1910. All of these publications were liberal, or freethinker, in emphasis, and circulation was small. *Cesky Oklahoman* claimed 1,200 subscribers, but evidence for the circulation of the others does not exist.

Oklahoma Czechs secured more long-lived press services from interests outside the state. In the early twentieth century there were two Czech firms, one in Chicago and one in Omaha, which were essentially small publishing empires. The Chicago firm, owned by the August Geringer family, published the freethinking daily *Svornost* (*"Harmony"*) and the valuable annual *Amerikan*. The other firm, founded by Jan Rosicky of Omaha, was the National Printing Company. Rosicky's most noteworthy efforts were the freethinking weekly *Pokrok Zapadu* (*"Progress of the West"*), the weekly *Osveta Amerika* (*"American Culture"*), and an agricultural journal, *Hospodar* (*"Husbandman"*). Both the Geringers and Rosicky established weekly local editions of their papers in Czech communities in Minnesota, Iowa, Nebraska, Kansas, the Dakotas, and Oklahoma. These local editions consisted of the ordinary format of their major papers, a page or two of local news supplied by a local correspondent, and a distinctive local name. There was nothing peculiarly Czech in this procedure. Small town and county English-language weeklies in many of the midwest and plains states were often metropolitan-produced "boilerplate" operations with local news added to blank space on the inside pages by a local editor or printer.

The Geringer firm was the first to enter the Oklahoma field. In 1905 *Oklahomske Noviny* (*"Oklahoma News"*), a semiweekly edition of *Svornost,* appeared in Oklahoma City. Its life span was approximately fifty years. With the resources of a major daily to sustain the operation, this paper contained instructional and amusement material in addition to political news and freethinking opinion. The Oklahoma City contributor for nearly half a century was Peter Rabstejnek, one of the most widely known early Czech settlers. Late in 1907 the Rosicky interests acquired *Cechoslovansky Obzor,* renamed it *Cesko-Slovansky Obzor,* and published the paper for several years as a local edition of *Osveta Amerika.*

Czech-language publication explicitly within and for Oklahoma ended before World War I. Aside from newspapers, publication in Oklahoma was not extensive. Apparently only two Czech-language books ever bore an Oklahoma imprint. The author of both was Frank Bronec of Richland. It is likely that part of his motivation was homesickness, for in 1906 he published an item called *Ceske koruny a o ceskem statu* (*"The Czech Crown Lands and the Czech State"*) and in 1908 he issued a tract with the wistful title *Stesk po stari vlast* (*"Longing for the Old Country"*). A last publishing effort in the Czech language in Oklahoma began in 1918 when Karel J. Sladek, a Pres-

Prague National Bank, about 1905–1907, Prague, Oklahoma. Courtesy of Mr. Joe Klabzuba.

byterian minister, moved his devotional monthly *Zivot* (*"Life"*) from Crete, Nebraska, to Oklahoma City. He continued to publish it there until 1922 when the magazine suspended.[4]

Journalism was of fundamental importance in the Czech-American community, but this generalization was less applicable to Oklahoma's Czech settlers. The opposite is true of Czech fraternalism and lodge activity in Oklahoma. If anything, Oklahoma Czechs over-represented themselves in fraternal affairs. Czechs are sociable, verbal, and argumentative people, and fraternal societies afford them an ideal outlet for these attributes. An anonymous observer of the Czechs in America once alleged that whenever two Czechs met two clubs soon appeared, both serving as forums for endless argumentation. There is nothing uniquely Czech about ethnic fraternalism. All nationality groups developed fraternal associations, and for nearly the same reasons. They are the collective outgrowth of tiny benefit societies created to afford immigrants financial protection against illness and death. Eventually the benefit societies consolidated, adopted professional procedures, and became modern life insurance companies serving a clientele usually limited to members of the relevant ethnic groups. Some, like the Polish National Alliance and the Sons of Italy, grew to gigantic size. Others, such as the Danish Brotherhood in America, never claimed more than a few thousand members. But the original local benefit society structures also survived, transformed into local lodge affiliates of the larger enterprises. At this level the activities are primarily social, but the members share a common ethnicity and the possession of similar insurance certificates.[5]

The larger Czech-American fraternal societies resulted from the energies of the freethinking Czechs. In a significant sense, moreover, they have old-world origins. Emigration from Bohemia and Moravia occurred in the context of economic modernization, major changes in landholding patterns, and great instability in the peasant villages. As the peasant villages crumbled, the villagers found it necessary to form protective institutions which extended beyond their immediate families. Associations appeared, based at first on a wider level of kinship, then embracing entire village populations, and finally involving entire regions. These associations often reappeared in America, and in the larger Czech communities benefit associations with membership requirements based upon village or region of origin were common. Hence the Czechs came to America with some experience in the management of protective institutions.[6]

Organizational consolidation occurred everywhere in American life in the last half of the nineteenth century, and Czech fraternal and benefit societies were part of this process. In fact, the Czechs were pioneers in ethnic fraternalism operating through the auspices of large-scale organizations. Fraternal organization began in 1854 when a group of early Czech settlers in St. Louis assembled in a saloon and created *Cesko-Slovansky Podporujici Spolek* ("Czech-Slavic Benevolent Society"), usually known as CSPS. This fraternal body was the principal constituent in a 1933 merger of fraternal groups which adopted the name of Czechoslovak Society of America. CSPS, the oldest ethnic benefit society in the United States, expanded beyond the St. Louis area and by the 1880s its lodges existed everywhere in Czech America. Beginning sometime in the 1870s the organization became a formal exponent of freethought, and Czech Catholics, though not excluded, normally refused to become involved with it.[7]

The principal function of CSPS was to provide financial benefits to the families of deceased members. It insured only males, but women participated as social members in the active social life of its growing number of lodges. Like many ethnic benefit societies, CSPS operated on the basis of a monthly assessment, depending on the mortality experience of the membership in the previous month. Such a system affords low-cost insurance only to a young membership, and Czechs from the older settlements east of the Mississippi began to die in increasing numbers in the 1890s. This provoked a policy division between the older eastern lodges and those in the plains states. Czechs in the West were normally younger than those in the eastern settlements, and they regarded the increasingly heavy assessments as unreasonable. Militants in the western lodges launched a campaign to put the insurance coverage on an actuarial basis with premiums based upon the ages of the policy holders. They also demanded full membership for women. CSPS officials refused the proposed changes, and in 1897 a western rebellion led to the secession of most of the western lodges and the creation of a new organization.

The secession of the western lodges of CSPS resulted in the formation in 1897 of *Zapadni Cesko-Bratrska Jednota* ("Western Bohemian Fraternal Association"), the principal institution in the lives of Oklahoma's Czechs from the year of its creation. Usually known by its initials, ZCBJ, this fraternal body adopted in 1971 a new and decidedly non-ethnic name, Western Fraternal Life Association.

The strategic figures in the establishment of ZCBJ were Nebraskans, especially the Omaha journalist Jan Rosicky, but the association has always maintained its insurance headquarters in Cedar Rapids, Iowa. Oklahoma Czechs did not participate in the formation of ZCBJ. But the only fraternal lodge operating in Oklahoma in 1897, CSPS Lodge No. 214 of Prague, quickly severed its ties with the parent body and affiliated with ZCBJ as Lodge Oklahoma No. 46. As one of the forty-nine lodges to secede by October 1897, the Prague organization enjoys "charter status" in ZCBJ, which soon became the largest of all Czech-American institutions.

The emergence of Czech communities in Oklahoma and the rapid development of ZCBJ occurred simultaneously in the pre-World War I years. ZCBJ grew rapidly until 1917, and women acquired full membership privileges at its first national convention. Over the years the leaders of ZCBJ displayed an admirable flexibility in adapting the organization to changing circumstances. As early as 1923 ZCBJ permitted the formation of English-speaking lodges, and a revision of membership requirements opened the organization to the non-Czech spouses of active members. Over the course of time this has altered the composition of the association considerably. In the current (1978) roster of ZCBJ lodges, nearly 500 in number, the number of non-Czech surnames in the list of lodge officials is strikingly large. It is now impossible to estimate how many of the 60,000 members of ZCBJ are of full Czech descent.

Czech Oklahoma has been within the ZCBJ sphere of influence since the foundation of the association. The Czechoslovak Society of America has no lodges in the state. Organization of Oklahoma's Czechs into ZCBJ lodges occurred largely before World War I, and with a few exceptions the lodge groups continue to exist, though not all have been continuously active. The lodges of ZCBJ in Oklahoma, and the pertinent details about them, are shown in the accompanying table.

Organization of ZCBJ groups in Oklahoma occurred primarily within a twenty-year period. One early lodge, organized in Renfrow, disbanded in 1904. Another lodge, which had the improbable name of "Oklahoma City Sooners No. 352," operated from 1934 to 1963. The headquarters of ZCBJ reported in 1972 that 283 of the association's lodges were active in that year. Twelve of the active lodges were in Oklahoma, and the state's Czechs hold their own in the ongoing activities of the association.[8]

Czechs of freethinking views dominated the ZCBJ lodges in

Oklahoma in the early days. Catholics did not ordinarily affiliate with the organization, and ZCBJ fulfilled many of the social and supportive functions usually associated with churches. The lodge became the central institution in the lives of many of Oklahoma's Czechs. After the birth of children, the lodge sponsored presentation ceremonies. Marriage ceremonies were lodge functions. Funerals were even more significant, and lodge officials conducted services, wives of lodge members provided food, and the membership in general offered assistance to bereaved families. Burials occurred in a lodge

Western Fraternal Life Association Lodges in Oklahoma

Location	Lodge Name	Date of Establishment
Prague	Oklahoma No. 46	1897
Perry	*Svornost* ("Harmony") No. 55	1898
Yukon	Jan Zizka No. 67	1899
Kingfisher	Kingfisher No. 88	1900
Oklahoma City	*Oklahomsky Rolnik* No. 89 ("Oklahoma Farmer")	1900
Oklahoma City	*Laska* ("Love") No. 109	1901
Garber	*Rovnost* ("Equality") No. 110	1901
Medford	Grant No. 134	1903
Willow	Granite No. 136	1903
Morrison	Ferdinand Lassalle No. 173	1907
Prague	*Samostatnost* ("Independence") No. 206	1910
Waukomis	*Vytrvalost* (Perseverance") No. 217	1910
Willow	Moravia No. 219	1910 (merged with Granite in 1914)
Willow	*Vitezslav* ("Victory") No. 248	1916
Oklahoma City	*Ceska Samostatnost* No. 250 ("Bohemian Independence")	1917 (merged with *Laska* in 1964)
Yukon	Yukon No. 281	1925 (merged with Jan Zizka in 1960)
El Reno	El Reno No. 438	1967

Sources: *Fraternal Herald ("Bratrsky Vestnik"),* 75 (July, 1972): 244–49; *Fraternal Herald,* 81 (February, 1978): 141. This magazine is the official publication of the Western Fraternal Life Association, ZCBJ.

cemetery, usually named "Czech National Cemetery." Such cemeteries exist in Oklahoma near Prague, in Oklahoma City, and elsewhere, monuments to the freethinking Czech settlers who dominated ZCBJ in its early days.[9]

Whenever lodges grew to a large size it was customary to construct a lodge hall. These facilities often became community centers, with musical, literary, and dramatic events occurring throughout the year. Dramatic presentations in the Czech language and Saturday night dances eased the arduous lives of the Czech farmers. In the summers the lodges for many years sponsored language schools for the children of the Czech settlers with the expectation that the Czech language would survive in the American West.

Typical of the larger ZCBJ lodges in Oklahoma is Lodge Jan Zizka No. 67 of Yukon, named in honor of the greatest Hussite general of the fifteenth century. Fewer than twenty settlers established the lodge in 1899, and the first members hosted the lodge activities in their homes. The members built a hall in 1901, replaced the original building with a larger structure in 1925, and made numerous additions and improvements in the 1950s. By 1908 the lodge had a dramatic club which performed Czech plays for the other lodge groups in Oklahoma until the early 1930s. A Czech summer language school, established in 1918, provided instruction for nearly twenty years. During World War II the lodge opened its weekly dances to all servicemen stationed in the Oklahoma City area and won a well-deserved reputation for hospitality. But the more ordinary activities of the lodge are the basis for its existence. Flowers grace the hospital rooms of its ill members, Christmas parties enliven the year for the children, and the families of deceased members receive the assistance that such times of crisis seem to require. The lodge donates to principal charities and shares the responsibility for maintaining four cemeteries. With nearly four hundred members in 1972, Lodge Jan Zizka is a typical American social service institution. For more than thirty years English has been the language of its monthly meetings and its other activities.[10]

Lodge *Vytrvalost* No. 217, whose members come from the agricultural settlements near Waukomis and Bison in Garfield County, is typical of the smaller lodges. Organized in 1910, the lodge roster was never large and currently lists forty-five members, nearly half of whom are over the age of sixty. Since fire destroyed the lodge hall in 1966, activities occur in the homes of members, and the deliberations of the members in their monthly meetings have been in

English since 1935. Though few children belong to the lodge, the principal service activity of the adult members is to support the Boy Scouts and Girl Scouts in the Garfield County area.[11]

Lodge Oklahoma No. 46 of Prague, the original Czech fraternal organization in Oklahoma, has a more distinctive history. Organized in 1897 by thirteen Czech settlers, all former members of a CSPS lodge, it currently claims a membership of 230, nearly 100 fewer than it had in the 1930s. In its long history this lodge group has offered, for Czechs and non-Czechs, more activities than any organization in the community. Aside from such specifically Czech activities as a language school, the lodge has sponsored guest speakers, dances, holiday celebrations, dramatic performances, athletics, political gatherings, concerts, picnics, benefit functions, weddings, and funerals. Its lodge hall has served as a community center even though only 20 percent of the area's residents are of Czech extraction.[12]

Over the years ZCBJ activities have extended far beyond the provision of insurance and relief services to distressed members. Lodge responsibilities always included the continuing education and cultural enrichment of the membership. The organization long ago lost any real connection with formal Freethought, and Catholics now comprise a large portion of its membership. Yet Czech fraternalism is not flourishing. With each generation there is attrition, and lodge life has a more obvious appeal for Czech Oklahomans of advanced years. Even the once formidable Lodge Oklahoma no longer sponsors children's activities, and its basic functions are now twofold—bingo and dancing.

In the period when Czech Oklahomans of Catholic convictions avoided ZCBJ, they developed a network of fraternal societies of their own. The creation of ZCBJ in 1897 represented a split in free-thinking Czech fraternalism and its reorientation along regional lines. The same kind of regional division characterized the Catholic fraternal institutions. Czech Catholics in the eastern states adhered to organizations like the Catholic Central Union and the National Alliance of Czech Catholics. In the west the Czech Catholics created an institution called *Katolicky Delnik,* now known by the English equivalent of its name, Catholic Workman. Founded in 1892 in New Prague, Minnesota, and still headquartered there, Catholic Workman has become the largest of all American fraternal institutions serving Catholics of Czech descent.

While ZCBJ is a self-contained organization, Catholic Workman is a part of the larger network of Catholic institutions. It is a layman's society with no connection to the clergy, organized originally for the same purposes as ZCBJ—the provision of fraternal insurance and the promotion of social activities. Its lodges have always existed as adjuncts to parishes and they have used the church facilities. Catholic Workman has no lodge halls of its own. Between 1900 and 1910 lodges of Catholic Workman were organized at Yukon, Prague, Mishak, Bison, and Hennessey. The Prague lodge faltered in the 1940s. Only the Yukon, Bison, and Oklahoma City (Mishak) lodges are presently active, and the old Mishak lodge, which has not been attached to a parish since St. Martin's burned in 1953, is the most active of all. Membership is small, and Catholic Workman has never posed a challenge to ZCBJ. The organization has about 200 adult members, fewer than any one of the larger ZCBJ lodges. According to the best information, Catholic Workman is not a particularly vital part of the Czech scene in Oklahoma.[13]

Both the press and the fraternal societies are normal kinds of American institutions, and their existence among Czech Americans is easy to understand. This is not true of *Sokol,* the third type of cultural institution established in Oklahoma by its Czech settlers. *Sokol* is more difficult to understand, and *Sokol* societies do not have equivalents in the larger society. On the surface it is merely a gymnastic society, and many *Sokols* also established gymnastic affiliates for girls and women known as *Sokolice.* In Czech the word means "falcon," and every member once wore a falcon feather in his official, fez-like hat. *Sokols* were often adjuncts to fraternal lodges, but in many of the larger Czech settlements they had separate organizations and halls.

Beneath the surface, however, *Sokol* is much more than an athletic organization. These clubs have promoted nationalistic, liberal, and educational ideals among the Czechs. Founded in Prague in 1862, *Sokol* was the creation of a classical scholar named Miroslav Tyrs and represented his belief in the Greek ideal of a "sound mind in a sound body." Tyrs thought that the fulfillment of such an ideal might play an important role in the Czech national revival of the nineteenth century, and his idea succeeded far beyond his expectations. The original idea also owed something to the earlier idea of the German *Turnverein* gymnastic societies, but the patriotic, nonathletic elements of *Sokol* were comparably more important than in the German clubs.[14]

Czech immigrants in St. Louis established the first *Sokol* in the United States in 1865. Within a generation two nationwide organizations existed, but in 1917 the two merged to form the American Sokol Organization with headquarters in Berwyn, Illinois. The idea also spread to other Slavic peoples, especially the Poles, and the Polish Falcons now comprise the largest *Sokol*-type organization in the United States. Czech *Sokol* became free-thought oriented early in its history, and the mainline organizations always reflected a middle-class bias. By the 1890s the recognition of these realities led to the establishment of competitor organizations. One was Catholic, the other Workingman's, but neither achieved the success or the permanence of the original societies.

Sokol philosophy required that each participant proceed through a number of stages in order to develop competence in two basic areas of gymnastics—free exercises (calisthenics) and apparatus. Later, games and other athletic skills entered the curriculum. The basic ideas were "training for everyone" and the development of equal skills in all activities. Each stage in *Sokol* training, especially for youth, also necessitated cultural activities in order to prepare the members for more rewarding lives. These societies always endeavored to create substantial libraries. Periodically, usually at five-year intervals, the *Sokol* clubs assemble in a central location for a *Slet,* a mass demonstration of the members' skills. Currently, there are plans to hold *Slet* XIV for the American *Sokols* in 1981 in Chicago.[15]

Sokol, with its nationalistic overtones, was more important to the Czechs in Bohemia than in the United States. Truly committed devotees ordinarily trained at least three evenings a week. For these reasons *Sokol* succeeded better in the urban colonies of American Czechs. It was, therefore, less important to the Czech farmers of Oklahoma than, for example, to the Czechs of Cleveland, Chicago, or Omaha. Yet the idea penetrated the Oklahoma Czech communities early in their histories. The Czechs in the Yukon area founded *Sokol Karel Havlicek* in 1898, one year earlier than the same settlers formed ZCBJ Lodge Jan Zizka. Since 1899 the two organizations have coexisted amicably, and the *Sokol* meets in the lodge hall. A second club, *Sokol Praha,* appeared in 1906 in Prague, Oklahoma. The second organization built its own facilities. There were also *Sokols,* now long abandoned, in Kingfisher and Oklahoma City.[16]

Sokol was a timely and worthy institution. Like so many ethnic organizations, it was difficult to sustain enthusiasm for it as one generation gave way to another. Prague's *Sokol Praha,* once under consideration to be designated as a national historical landmark, succumbed instead to the wrecker's ball in 1976. Its officials donated the gymnastic equipment to the local school system. *Sokol Karel Havlicek* still exists in Yukon, but gymnastic activity is not in evidence.[17] Over the years *Sokol* has become more social, less idealistic, and certainly less athletic. The activities of local units often consist of bazaars, covered-dish suppers and pancake breakfasts. Many units, especially in the plains states, have disbanded since World War II. The American Sokol Organization is only a shadow of what it was at the height of its influence a half century ago. This is unfortunate, for Sokol's effects were surely beneficial. During World War II, for example, the national rejection rate for inductees into military service was nearly 50 percent. For youth trained in *Sokol* it was less than 1 percent.[18]

The Czechs of Oklahoma have always been a small group living far from the major centers of Czech-American activity. For this reason many Czech institutions had no impact on the local Czechs. The Society for the Promotion of Higher Education, an organization formed in 1902 by Czechs in the Middle West, had no affiliates in

Building the *Sokol* Hall in Prague, Oklahoma, about 1902–1906. Courtesy of Mrs. Lizzie Jezek.

45

Oklahoma. The same was true of the Komensky Educational Clubs which flourished on many college campuses in the 1920s and 1930s. The Czechoslovak National Council of America and the Czech-American Alliance have had little, if any, influence in Oklahoma. The Czechoslovak Society of Arts and Sciences in America, founded in 1957, has only one Oklahoma member. Only the last institution has real national significance at the moment. The Czech-American organizations which do function in the state, however, are typical American social service institutions. They are distinguished from the larger complex of social institutions by the peculiarity of their origins, the longevity of some "old settler" members, and the revival of ethnic consciousness which began to influence American society in the 1960s.

Chapter 6

CZECH OKLAHOMANS
AND AGRICULTURE

In 1971 the Grant County Historical Society issued a local history which contained the life stories of many of the old settlers in the county. Among these little biographies was an account of Joseph Skrdla, who reminisced about his life in 1960 when he was eighty-eight. Born in 1872 in Bohemia, Skrdla came to Nebraska with his parents as a small boy. As a young man of twenty-one he made the run of 1893 into the Cherokee Strip on a ten-dollar pony. He located a claim near Renfrow, just south of the Kansas border, and built a dugout for his first home. In recalling the principal events of his long life he remembered the eight years of service he obtained from a discarded cookstove and the old-time prices of steak, flour, kerosene, and California wine. He married a Czech girl, Millie Buresh, in 1899, and the newlyweds spent an unusual honeymoon. They sank two wells on their property—he dug and his bride raised the soil and lowered rocks for the walls. The Skrdlas eventually reared five children, acquired their first automobile in 1916, and developed a fondness for travel and antique clocks. But mostly, Joseph Skrdla remembered that he farmed.[1]

A few years later Bessie Dvorak, an elderly widow living in Stillwater, told an interviewer the story of her life. Born Busina Kosnar in 1895 in Pustina, Bohemia, Mrs. Dvorak came to Perry, Oklahoma, in 1906. In Czech *pustina* means "wilderness," and the move to Perry was more than a journey from the Old World to the New. It was a transition from an old wilderness to a new wilderness. About life in Bohemia before her family emigrated she recalled only that her father was mayor of his village at the time of their departure, the elaborate village funeral of her grandfather, baking bread in a large brick oven, and making noodles. About life in Oklahoma she remembered five years of elementary schooling, legally Americanizing her given name to Bessie, her marriage to Frank Dvorak, whose family lived on an adjacent farm, the birth and rearing of four children, and work in the fields. But mostly, Bessie Dvorak remembered that she farmed.[2]

And in 1976 the Alfalfa County Historical Society published a county history which contained a biography of Frank Pecha, who died in 1967 at the age of ninety-five. Born in 1871 in Bohemia, Pecha emigrated in 1874 with his family to Valparaiso, Nebraska. In 1893 he made the run into the Cherokee Strip in a spring wagon and entered a claim near Goltry. Pecha's first home was a dugout. Later he built a sod house and followed that with a one-room frame dwelling which he gradually expanded. He married a Czech immigrant, Christina Dragoun, but only two of the six children born to the marriage survived the terrors which the prairie visits upon its human occupants. And in 1914 a cyclone destroyed his home and all of its contents. Rebuilding was laborious, but Frank Pecha endured. His landholdings grew to 630 acres, and a third generation of Pecha's family now resides on the original claim. Pecha surely survived more than normal adversity. But mostly, in his long life, he farmed.[3]

Joseph Skrdla, Bessie Dvorak, and Frank Pecha probably never met each other, but they had much in common. They were typical of Oklahoma's Czech pioneers, and their lives were simple. They farmed. These two words provide both a memoir and an epitaph for the first generation of Czech Oklahomans and a large majority of their descendants. To the sophisticated, modern, urban American the lives of these farmers may seem quaint or even foolish, but the opportunity to farm meant the fulfillment of life's goals for each of them. Not only did the Czech settlers in Oklahoma farm, they did so diligently, successfully, and permanently. What accounts for their success? Why could Czech farmers carve a living from the reluctant prairie, endure dust, drought, and cyclone, and survive the Dust Bowl calamity when so many other farmers abandoned the land? John Steinbeck did not write *Grapes of Wrath* about Czech Oklahomans.

Obviously, Czechs were not good farmers merely because they were Czechs. There were shiftless and improvident Czech farmers in the homeland and in America. But they were not, and are not, very numerous, and the reasons lie buried in that peculiar assortment of values and attitudes known as Czech culture. There was a relationship between Czech rural culture, or peasant culture, and agriculture

The Louis Hanska family on their Shell Creek farm, three miles west of Yukon, Oklahoma, about 1918. Left to right, Raymond, Louis, Richard (baby), Victoria and Evelyn. Evelyn was four years old. Courtesy of Mrs. Louis Hanska and the Western History Collections, University of Oklahoma.

which was evident even on the plains of Oklahoma. A case study conducted in the 1930s illustrated this relationship clearly. Russell Lynch, an agricultural economist from Oklahoma A. and M. College, undertook an intensive study of the Czech-American farmers in the vicinity of Prague, probably the most concentrated body of Czech agriculturalists in the state. His conclusions were more than laudatory about Czech farming practices. They were plainly flattering.[4]

Russell Lynch used an analytical method common in the social sciences. He chose a large sample of Czech farmers and compared their agricultural performance in numerous categories of behavior with the performance of the members of three randomly chosen "control groups" of "native" farmers. The subjects of his study, Czechs and "natives," all farmed in the same part of Lincoln County and engaged in the same kind of farming. Lynch learned that there was more to the success of the Czech farmers than a capacity for hard work, although one observer of Czech farmers on the plains did ascribe their success to the fact that they "knew how to work harder and live on less than any American born settler."[5]

Both Czechs and "natives" settled in Lincoln County at the same time, in the 1891 run into the Sac and Fox lands. Except for a limited amount of bottomland, the soils in the Prague area were not of prime quality, and the area's terrain was rugged. Leaching and erosion were soon evident in the area, though by 1910 the county became the leading cotton growing county in Oklahoma. The county's eminence in cotton production was short-lived. In less than half a century the area passed through the familiar cycle of cotton and corn to widespread land abandonment. But the "native" element abandoned the land. In the Dust Bowl years the natives were twenty times more likely to leave than the Czechs. In contrast to the "natives," the Czechs had every reason to stay. As Lynch pointed out, they had "farms in good condition, well-painted homes, neatly kept; and more than the average number of outbuildings. They have a varied and interesting social life. They give their sons and daughters educational opportunities. They have money in the bank."[6] The Czechs averaged more than twenty-seven years on their farms, or from 30 to 50 percent longer than the natives in the control groups. They were a third less likely to be tenants rather than owners. Fully two-thirds of the Czechs who were tenant farmers had a blood relationship to their landlords. They did indeed have money in the bank—more per capita than any people in Oklahoma.

Aside from stability and tenancy rates, how did the Czech farmers differ from the natives? Did *on the farm* agricultural practices explain why the Czechs found it worthwhile to stay while the "natives" left, though both groups faced the same realities of climate and soil? There were such practices, which derived from the attitudes dictated by culture. The first relevant practice was in land use. Czechs cultivated more acres per farm than the "natives," and they were much more likely to fertilize the land. Part of the additional acreage utilized by the Czech farmers provided oats to feed the farm animals, and part of the acreage afforded an opportunity to grow more cotton as a cash crop. Czechs grew more feed and cover crops than the natives. At the same time they devoted fewer acres to clean-tilled crops like corn and grain sorghums, thus reducing the potential of serious erosion on their farms. They were also more likely to practice crop rotation. In short, the Czechs did a better job in caring for the soil and securing income for their efforts.

In addition, the Czech farmers were more likely to maintain milk cows, to keep orchards, to cultivate gardens, and to own work stock and hogs. They normally preserved their own meat products and prepared their own lard, while the natives did not. Besides the fresh fruit obtained from orchards, on many Czech farms some of the fruit ended up in the potable and fermented form upon which both law

Karel D. Bicha

The Louis Hanska family harvesting wheat on the Shell Creek farm during the 1930s Depression. In the background is a Fortson tractor, one of the first in Oklahoma. Courtesy of Mrs. Louis Hanska and the Western History Collections, University of Oklahoma.

and custom in Oklahoma frowned. A primary garden crop was cabbage, destined to be "stomped" in the sauerkraut barrel. None of these ingredients of self-sufficiency characterized the farms of the "natives."

In the 1920s many of the Czechs in the Prague area began to receive additional revenue from the discovery of oil in the area. It was common among the Czechs to use this revenue to improve their farm plants, not to depart for a life of ease off the farm. Hence Russell Lynch found that the Czechs had larger homes than members of the "native" control groups, maintained these homes in better condition, and extended the same principles to their outbuildings. And the Czechs had more homes equipped with running water, electricity, indoor toilet facilities, and radios. They were less inclined to own automobiles than the natives, preferring instead to use farm trucks for both business and pleasure. In summary, the Czechs in the Prague area were more affluent, more comfortable, and more self-sufficient than the "natives." Why?

Cultural factors explain the success of the Czech farmers. These factors were not peculiar to the Czechs alone, and most of them apply to other nationality groups with roots in central or eastern Europe. In the first place, the Czechs were a product of a collective peasant environment, and the Czech settlers in Oklahoma still reflected a European peasant mentality. One reality dominated peasant life—

51

there was never enough of anything. This reality produced at least one commandment in addition to the original ten: thou shalt not waste. Neither land, nor livestock, nor time existed to be wasted. Every foot of land had its uses, every part of a slaughtered animal had its uses, every moment of the working day had its uses. Russell Lynch duly noted the excellence of land use by the Czech farmers, but he missed the other elements. An acquaintance with Czech blood sausage or liver sausage would have opened other areas of investigation to him.

A primary cultural factor which insured the agricultural success of Czech farmers was their attitude toward the land itself. It was very different from that which prevailed on the American frontier. It was affectionate, reverent, almost worshipful. Land deserved to be conserved and nurtured, not assaulted and abandoned. Czech-American farmers did not oppose mobility. If they had believed in cultivating the same land forever they would not have come to Oklahoma. But they believed in mobility, in order to achieve permanence, not for the sake of assuring "elbow room." For centuries the Czechs had lived with the implications of land scarcity, and this reality conditioned them to the necessity for both conservation and self-sufficiency. Land ownership was a visible sign of success to the Czechs. In America even retired Czech farmers tried to retain some land because it meant status and security to them. To Czechs the land was not for exploitation but for permanence.

The idea of community also assured the success and stability of the Czechs as farmers. In spite of the deep divisions in Czech America on religious and social questions, Czech farmers established a workable sense of community on agricultural and economic matters. On vital agricultural issues they did not allow divisions in the community to retard progress and the exchange of ideas. The Czechs originally lived in peasant villages which were true communities. All of the human contacts of the inhabitants occurred within the context of these villages. It was not possible to reestablish peasant villages in America, but it was possible to duplicate some of their functions. In Prague, Oklahoma, for example, the Czech farmers of the surrounding countryside used the ZCBJ lodge or the church in the village as the focus of their social existence and achieved a close association with the activities of the community. They did not distinguish between village and countryside, and did not regard the village inhabitants with distrust. Czech farmers played important roles in the public and social life of the village. By way of contrast,

The Barta Hotel, Prague, Oklahoma. Mrs. Barta, seated far right, named the town of Prague. Courtesy of Mr. Conrad Knoepfli.

the "native" farmers in Russell Lynch's control groups had no such attitude toward or contact with the village of Prague. They viewed it in a detached and distrustful way, as a place to trade and secure needed services. They deprived themselves of social life and of a sense of belonging. But the Czech farmers participated actively in the affairs of the village from the outset. For example, when the imminent arrival of the Ft. Smith and Western Railroad in 1902 led to the creation of Prague, it seemed that the new village needed a hotel. A Czech farmer named Frank Barta moved a farm house onto a village site and the village had its hotel! It remained in operation until 1961.[7]

Another aspect of the idea of community gave stability to the Czech farmers of Oklahoma. Owing to historical factors Czech culture was unusually democratic. There were few class distinctions among the people. Czechs refused to formalize the differences between landowners and tenant farmers, and they did not regard tenants in the Czech group as inferiors. Most Czech tenants, at least in the Prague area, were relatives of the owners, but nonetheless the absence of class differences helped tenants to achieve a sense of belonging which "native" tenants lacked. And Czech farmers who remained in tenant status did not evoke scorn or condemnation from their more successful neighbors but received expressions of sympathy for their bad luck.

An interesting example of democratic procedures among Czech farmers was a device called a "beef club." Each week a designated farmer, selected on a rotating basis from among the club members, supplied a steer for slaughter. The butcher received compensation in the form of fresh beef, and each of the members secured the cuts which he ordered. At the end of a season those who used more beef than they supplied settled their accounts in cash. Those who supplied more than they used received compensation in cash. Club members benefited greatly from such an arrangement. Tax collectors did not.[8]

A final cultural factor insured the success of the Czechs as farmers, one which many observers have neglected. Until recently, at least, the Czechs employed a different division of labor on their farms. This had its roots in the peasant culture of Central Europe, and was not peculiar to the Czechs. Since Czech farms in Oklahoma were so productive and self-sufficient, labor was plentiful. On the average Czech families were large, but this fact alone does not suffice to explain productivity on the farm. Czech farmers delegated routine farm tasks to their children, perhaps earlier in their lives than was customary among the native farmers, and these tasks took precedence over all competing interests. During his youth on the Nebraska frontier, Addison E. Sheldon, a former superintendent of the Nebraska Historical Society, taught some of the Czechs who eventually settled in Oklahoma. He recalled that at a certain time in the year the Czech children were always absent from school. Their parents believed deeply in education, but cornhusking came first.[9]

The productive labor of children on the Czech farms was not as important as another aspect of the division of labor. On the Czech farm field work was men's work—and women's work. On the farms of the natives, irrespective of whether their origins were Yankee or southern, field work was man's work. In Bohemia and Moravia peasant women routinely worked in the fields, distinguishable at a distance from the men only by their bright red head shawls. The same cultural precedent applied among Czechs in America, and more manpower was utilized on the Czech farms with "womanpower." By way of contrast, the example of the young widow of Yankee origins, compelled to do field work on a prairie farm because of her unfortunate circumstances, is the stuff of which television heroines are made. It represented a departure from native cultural tradition. But Czech women were often among the corn and the cabbages.

The Czech farmers of Oklahoma were never totally out of step with the commercial agriculture that developed around them. As time went on and one generation gave way to another, Czech farms became more specialized and less self-sufficient. This was especially true where winter wheat and livestock grazing emerged dominant—Grant, Noble, Garfield, and Kingfisher counties. It was also true to a lesser extent of the Yukon and El Reno areas in Canadian County, although proximity to metropolitan Oklahoma City produced a different kind of specialization. The Prague area remained the most diversified or nonspecialized, where a balanced emphasis on corn, cattle, grain sorghums, and alfalfa gradually became the accepted pattern. Cotton growing and dairying, once common around Prague, are no longer important.[10]

Farming dominated Czech life in Oklahoma from the time of the first settlements. Not all of Oklahoma's Czech settlers were farmers, of course. There were businessmen and a few professional people, including at least one physician, among the first settlers in 1889–1890. But the great majority of the nonfarming Czechs were craftsmen engaged in trades closely related to agriculture. They were harnessmakers, butchers, blacksmiths, and machinists. Among

John Francis Kroutil. From Rex Harlow, *Oklahoma Leaders.* Courtesy of the Western History Collections, University of Oklahoma.

those who secured the capital for enterprise on a larger scale, lumber and agricultural implement businesses predominated. In Prague, for example, the Czechs operated more than a fourth of the village's eighty businesses, and all of them except the restaurant and the tailor shop had a close relationship to the farm community.[11] Currently, one of the largest tractor dealerships in the United States is owned by a Czech American in Kremlin, Oklahoma.

The most notable of the agriculture-related success stories in Czech Oklahoma were undoubtedly the flour milling enterprises of the Kroutil and Dobry families of Yukon. John Kroutil was especially prominent among the members of these two intermarried but competing milling families. Born in 1875 in Prague, Bohemia, Kroutil was the oldest son in a prominent Czech business family. The family freighting business was bankrupted by the Austro-Prussian War and the Kroutils emigrated in 1882 to Wahoo, Nebraska. Young John Kroutil came to Yukon in 1890 and established himself as a farmer and grain trader. He acquired an elevator and eventually a small mill, and built the mill into a multimillion-dollar enterprise. By 1928 "Yukon's Best," the family trade name, was prominent in the Southwest. John Kroutil became president of both the state and the regional milling associations, engaged in philanthropic activities, organized the Yukon National Bank, and dabbled in Democratic party affairs. But it was successful farming which afforded men like Kroutil their business opportunities.[12]

Chapter 7
FAMILY AND SOCIAL LIFE

Czech Oklahomans, like all Czech Americans, tried their best to preserve the values, family customs, and social forms of the Czech folk tradition. These cultural peculiarities evolved in the peasant villages of Bohemia and Moravia over the course of centuries, and like the folkways of all peoples they were resistant to change. The tendency of Czech settlers to create ethnic colonies, and the extraordinary emphasis on the privacy of the family in the larger American culture, afforded the Czechs an opportunity for cultural preservation without parallel in the western world. Though the folkways of the Czechs appeared strange and even offensive to some Americans, many of them persisted until the passage of generations and the normal processes of assimilation took their toll.

The basic circumstances of Czech emigration guaranteed the maintenance of some family and social customs. In the emigration of most nationality groups from central and eastern Europe to the United States young, single males and married men who hoped to send for their families after they established themselves in America were the normal migrants. Among the Czechs the family unit predominated from the beginning. By the time of the secondary migration of Czechs to Oklahoma the family was even more dominant as the unit of settlement. The Czech family in Oklahoma was not different in structure or behavior from Czech families in other states in which farming was the basic occupation of the settlers. Families were probably smaller than the normal peasant families in Bohemia and Moravia, but they were larger on average than "native" American families. Family units with five to ten children were common among the first generation of Czech Oklahomans. After the first generation, family size normally declined.[1] This decline in the birthrate, of course, was a typical characteristic of twentieth-century families and occurred in the Czech lands as well as among all groups in the United States. Moreover, in Bohemia and Moravia the birth of children was surrounded by elaborate folk rituals and customs—the lying-in of the mother, formal and structured godparenthood, and a final ceremony which occurred about six weeks after birth known as the "churching" of the mother. Emigration weakened these village customs; most of them disappeared after a few years in the American environment.[2]

In its internal structure and division of power the Czech family had certain unique characteristics. It was, like most families of European origin, both father-headed and mother-centered. But it was different in this way. Father-headed did not mean father-dominated, for unlike the families of other Slavic nationalities, the Czech family was not a patriarchy. The father's authority was not exclusive, and the mother's power was considerable. The Czech father never undertook a major venture or made a crucial decision without prolonged consultation with his wife. Perhaps this peculiarity was a result of the classlessness of Czech culture which evolved after the native nobility became extinct in the seventeenth century. It was also a by-product of the Czech woman's capabilities in the performance of the same farm tasks as men.

Nevertheless, the role of the Czech father was primarily that of breadwinner and disciplinarian. Unlike the American family, close emotional relationships between a father and his offspring were not customary. The family itself was parent-centered, and old-time Czech Americans would find the child-centeredness of the modern American family absolutely incomprehensible. Paternal discipline was ordinarily harsh—excessively so by contemporary standards. One common disciplinary tool was a device called a *dutky,* a leather whip similar to a cat-o'-nine-tails or the quirt once used by horsewomen. In many Czech families the *dutky* hung on a wall in the family home as a symbol of paternal authority long after the children had grown up and departed. Even today the Czech-American family exhibits an unusual degree of parent-centeredness.[3]

On the other hand, the wife and mother in the Czech-American family was a power in her own right. There were few, if any, family secrets, and the woman's input in decision making was important. Czech-American women, both in urban circumstances and on farms, did not have easy lives. Not only did they bear and nurture many children, but they worked hard in the fields, or the shops, or sometimes in tenement or factory crafts under unhealthful conditions. Yet Czech men were not averse to or embarrassed by some domestic responsibilities. In the early twentieth century, for example, a New York social worker surprisingly found Czech husbands at work doing the family wash and not chagrined in the least to be performing such routine household tasks.[4] But the kitchen was the woman's exclusive domain. Edward Steiner, a Jewish immigrant from Austria, was one of the boldest commentators on immigrant life in early twentieth-century America. Steiner did not like the Czechs very much. But he admitted that "the Czech has a reputation as an epicure, and the Bohemian girl is generally an excellent cook, in addition to her other good qualities."[5] Steiner might have added that these excellent cooks spent long periods of time in the kitchen, for Czech cooking is very time consuming. Anglo-Saxon women spent much less time in the preparation of food. The differential results were predictable. The Czechs have a noteworthy culinary tradition, while Anglo-Saxon cuisine is perhaps the most elementary in the western world.

The children of Oklahoma's Czech settlers also differed somewhat from native American children. Differences in behavior and customs, and peculiarities in their use of English, sometimes provoked other children to call them "bohunk."[6] There is no evidence that they experienced any special discrimination, but they assimilated slowly. Long periods of farm work deprived them of opportunities for contact with "native" children, for early in life Czech children received specific farm duties. They probably commenced their working lives earlier than American children, and they worked under disciplining and isolated conditions in many cases. The circumstances of their lives also had some positive effects. A number of authorities observed that Czech children rarely posed discipline problems at school. Nor did the ordered nature of their lives seem to dampen their enthusiasm. One former Yankee schoolmaster, for example, recalled that some Czech children were dull, but recalled none who were not enthusiastic. Angie Debo remembered the Czech children of the Bison-Hennessey area as capable young people.[7] Yet under different and more assimilated circumstances they might have had more ample opportunities.

Certain other conditions inherent in Czech culture also shaped the behavior of the Czech family in Oklahoma. One of the most fundamental of these related to the treatment of aging parents. It was normal for Czech farmers who reached a particular age to turn control of the farm over to one of their children, ordinarily the eldest son. When this occurred, the farmer immediately lost much of his status and power. By custom that dated back to medieval times and which survived in America in altered form, the retiring farmer usually negotiated the retention of certain privileges with his son, or daughter, and successor. These included the right to room and board for himself and his wife in the family home, medical care, and sometimes a share of the crops. Often these agreements took written form. While these formal agreements usually did not persist beyond the second generation in America, they were not uncommon in Czech-American farm families even in the 1940s. In Oklahoma, however, both land values and the mineral rights attached to much Czech-owned land dictated more complicated disposal methods.[8]

Another normal attribute of Czech-American farm families was the disposition to create enclaves of family and kinfolk. These attracted fellow Czechs, and with the passage of time and a sufficient number of offspring they became true colonies. The colonies achieved a permanent or ongoing characteristic as adult members insisted their children marry within the Czech group. Population experts call this intermarriage process "endogamy," and Czech Oklahomans were conspicuously endogamous for perhaps two generations. Endogamy created a strong sense of security and refuge, but it obviously retarded assimilation. It had both positive and negative effects which, like many cultural attributes, probably balance in the final analysis. It is no longer the norm for Czech Oklahomans.[9]

Many of the characteristics of the Czech-Oklahoman family, therefore, resulted from the adaptation of European customs. The effects were both good and bad. Dependency and consequent demands upon public welfare programs have been rare among Czech Americans. Broken homes were also rare, and children were infrequently delinquent. But Czechs were not the most popular of settlers, partly because of their clannishness and partly because of behavior traits which were all too common among them—quarrelsomeness, suspiciousness, and an inclination to carry small disagreements beyond the point of reason. All of these traits were typical of peoples with peasant backgrounds. Another charge often leveled against Czechs was that they were excessively materialistic and disposed to haggle endlessly over the prices of nearly everything. There was considerable truth in this allegation. Materialism in America was hardly the exclusive domain of Czech Americans. But anyone who has observed the behavior of a large number of old Czech settlers can testify to the peculiarly hard nature of their material concerns. Edward Steiner called the materialism of Czech Americans their "greatest sin." The famous social reformer Jane Addams explained it in terms of typical Slavic land hunger.[10]

In many respects Czech life in both Europe and America was more social than familial in its orientation, because the roots of most Czechs lay in villages that rarely contained more than 200 people. Intermarriage within the village or within a group of closely connected villages was the rule, and village populations were often little more than extended families. The closeness and the convivial social relations that characterized the village in the Czech lands were impossible to duplicate in America. But the dense network of clubs, lodges and benefit societies of Czech America represented an attempt to adapt the sociability of Czech village life to the new land.

The basic social institution in every Czech village was the inn or *hospoda.* Every Czech village had one or two inns, which served as the social centers of the villages. Men visited them daily, women used them occasionally. The male villager who failed to appear at the inn acquired a reputation as unsociable and tightfisted. The inn was primarily a drinking and dancing establishment, but it was not the equivalent of the English pub or the American saloon. In America Czechs had only the saloon to patronize, and it assumed a large role in their lives. Some of the important Czech-American organizations had their origins in saloons.[11]

All of the foregoing serves to establish an elementary fact of Czech-American life. In family circumstances, and especially in social situations, the Czechs were, and are, a "wet" ethnic group. Alcoholic beverages play an important role in Czech life. This meant that in states like Oklahoma, which prohibited alcoholic beverages in most forms for more than half a century, the social inclinations of the Czech Oklahomans and the reality of public policy were at odds. Primarily, and fortunately from the point of view of Oklahoma policy, Czechs are principally beer drinkers. Such beloved terms in the vocabulary of the brewing art as "pilsener" and "budweiser" have Bohemain origins. Czechs are also moderate consumers of wine, and the grape-vines commonly found on Czech-Oklahoman farms furnish more than fresh fruit. On occasion Czechs also imbibed a fiery liquid called *slivovice,* a brandy distilled from plum wine. When Oklahoma became a state in 1907 both the saloon and the open dispensing of alcoholic beverages became illegal. Undoubtedly the social spirit of Oklahoma's Czech settlers suffered. But their spirit never suffered from a lack of spirits. It was a rare Czech housewife whose skills did not include the preparation of home brew. It was a rarer Czech man who was deficient in the art of wine making.

While Czech culture was a drinking culture, it was even more a musical and dancing culture. Proficiency in the playing of musical instruments was probably commoner among the Czechs than among any other people in the world, and this truth occasioned an old cliche, "a Czech, a musician."[12] The violin, accordion, clarinet, tuba, and the guitar-like string instruments which have many variants in Slavic culture areas were the usual instruments. In hundreds of American communities before the 1920s the "leetle Sherman pand" which entertained the local residents was more likely to be composed of Czechs than Germans.

But playing musical instruments was not an end in itself. It was supposed to facilitate dancing, and dancing is extraordinarily important in Czech-American social life. There were once literally hundreds of Czech folk dances, many of them originating in southern Bohemia, the part of the Czech lands which contributed the largest number of immigrants to the United States. Many of these folk dances were elaborate and required devoted preparation. For this reason most of them did not long survive in America. But this was hardly true of the most notable of all Czech dances—the polka. Originating about 1830 in Bohemia, the polka soon became an international dance form. The name "polka" comes from the Czech word *pulka* or "half-step." It penetrated the culture of the German lands and achieved popularity among most of the Slavic peoples. The polka soon evolved into a number of related dance forms which varied by nationality. Oklahoma's Czech pioneers brought the dance with them, and both the polka and the polka band, dominated by accordion, clarinet, and tuba, have flourished ever since in most of the Czech settlements. Some of Oklahoma's Czech polka bands, such as the Masopust and Belsky bands of Oklahoma County, achieved more than local fame. A Czech polka club with several hundred members still enjoys a flourishing existence.[13]

Good food in more than ample quantities is also central to Czech Society. No matter how precarious the family's financial condition, it would not occur to a good Czech to cut corners on the food budget. Czech cuisine shows strong traces of German influence, and many culinary items—sausages, sauerkraut, and strudel, for example—are as much Czech as German. The cuisine has two essential features: it is heavy and filling, and its preparation requires a large expenditure of time. Among the more common items are the three "national" dishes, roast goose, roast duck, and roast pork. Various goulashes and an array of sausages, including blood sausage and liver sausage, are also standard fare. The usual accompaniments of the meat dishes are dumplings, or *knedliky,* which also come in a number of varieties, sauerkraut, and a light rye bread laced with caraway seed. The bakery, however, makes the Czech culinary tradition most distinctive. Strudels, fruit filled buns called *buchty,* and bite-sized pastry containing fruit, poppy seed, cheese or nuts, known as *kolace,* or *kolacky,* are the most ordinary items. Finally, Czechs utilize a number of spices which are not customarily used in the "native" American cooking tradition— garlic, caraway, poppy seed, dill, anise, paprika, saffron, marjoram and bay leaf.

Czech Americans have always placed a great deal of emphasis upon the pleasures of consumption. In the self-denying atmosphere of evangelical Protestant Oklahoma their values sometimes conflicted with the majority attitude. Festivals and celebrations were nearly continuous in the Czech villages, but since most of them had meaning only within the village setting they did not survive the transatlantic migration. This lessened the potential for misunderstanding between

The wedding picture of Victoria Novak and Louis Hanska, March 18, 1914. She is wearing a tangerine dress and an artificial corsage. Courtesy of Mrs. Louis Hanska and the Western History Collections, University of Oklahoma.

63

Czech Oklahomans and their neighbors. But one central Czech social custom did survive quite well in America, though it survived in trimmed-down form. This was the wedding.

In the evangelical Protestant culture of Oklahoma a normal wedding consisted of a brief ceremony followed by a short celebration with coffee and cake. An old-fashioned wedding celebration in a Czech village took three days to complete, and feasting was more or less continuous. It was an important event because it involved the transfer of property and, in a sense, the welfare of the entire village. Such elaborate nuptial procedures did not survive among the Czechs in Oklahoma. Other Czech marriage customs, such as the choice of mates by the parents, the use of marriage brokers, and the oral announcement of an invitation to a wedding by a master of ceremonies, had no place at all in America. Yet the wedding was and is a most important social event in Czech communities, and such customs as prolonged eating and drinking and the wedding dance continue to characterize these affairs.

Many, if not most, of the distinctive family and social customs of the Czechs in America have faltered in the past generation or two. Fifty years ago a Yankee observer could write of the Czechs' "joyous and sometimes hilarious beer hall festivals, their old-country music, their strange, intense language with its jarring z's and r's."[14] This is no longer true. Czech social institutions primarily attract the elderly, and the saloon is no factor at all.

Chapter 8

CZECH OKLAHOMANS,
PAST AND PRESENT

It is possible for a casual tourist to travel the length and breadth of Oklahoma and remain unaware of the existence of white ethnic groups in the state's population. A more careful observer will soon discover that Oklahoma's borders contain a rich and varied human mosaic. To a diligent inquirer the rewards of exploring this human panorama are considerable. Czech Americans are only a small part of Oklahoma's diverse population. Yet one cannot view the imposing hulks of the old Kroutil and Dobry flour mills which straddle U.S. Highway 66 in Yukon, or scan the prairie horizon in Canadian, Kingfisher, Grant, Garfield, and Noble counties where the neat farmhouses of Czech Americans sit in the midst of fields of winter wheat and grazing land filled with cattle, without realizing that the Czechs have contributed much to the state. As the president of the Prague National Bank phrased it recently, the Czechs have done "tolerably well" in Oklahoma.[1]

Prosperity did not come easily. Czech life in Oklahoma began on homesteads and "relinquishments," and more often than not the first homes of the settlers were sod houses or dugouts. Most of the Czechs came to Oklahoma with very little. Some came with even less. In *Prairie City* Angie Debo told the story of Anton Jezek, who settled in the 1890s on a claim between Hennessey and Marshall in Kingfisher County. Occasionally Jezek came into Marshall to purchase supplies. Even in the summer heat he always wore a tightly buttoned coat and a red kerchief around his neck. Years later Jezek's grandchildren explained why he dressed so uncomfortably. He was a modest man, and for the first two years of his life in Oklahoma he did not own a shirt. But Anton Jezek survived, and his grandson was the first Czech to graduate from high school in Marshall.[2] He also had an appropriate surname for a prairie farmer. In Czech, *jezek* is the name of a spiked farm implement utilized to crush tough clods of soil.

The story of Antonie Petru Vaverka is also instructive. In 1905 she arrived in Okeene, Oklahoma Territory, accompanied only by an older brother. She was ten years old, and never saw her parents again. She did not come voluntarily but was sent to assist an aging great-aunt on her farm. She was unaware of her destination, or that her services had been pledged to her relative for five years. Traveling on a ship with immigrants and cattle, upon which all of the passengers except her brother spoke only German, Antonie Petru came to Oklahoma in tears. She cried *en route* to America and for many years thereafter. She cried when immigration officials relieved her of the two fine silk scarves she was carrying as presents to her Oklahoma relative. She cried when the American school children in Okeene poked fun at her inability to speak English. She hid in a barn to avoid school and the abuse of her classmates. When she was fourteen the death of her great-aunt released her from family servitude. But she was alone in the world, and the only work she could find was in a local boarding house as domestic help at 50 cents a week. Eventually an order of nuns in Guthrie took her in, and amid long hours of work in the kitchen the sisters taught her the English language. Finally, she went to Bison, Garfield County, to help her brother on his farm. There she met and married Frank Vaverka, another Czech settler, and she stopped crying. Antonie Vaverka also survived. She still lives in Bison, a robust widow in her mid-eighties.[3]

Most of Oklahoma's Czech settlers came to the new land under less distressing circumstances. They secured farmland, nurtured it, and fulfilled their personal goals. A few of them rose to positions of prominence in their communities. The career of Peter Rabstejnek of Oklahoma City affords a good illustration of the public success of a Czech Oklahoman. Born in 1874 in Kozlany, Bohemia, he emigrated to the United States in 1894, and lived for brief periods in New York, Chicago, and Table Rock, Nebraska. He came to Oklahoma in 1898 and worked as a tenant farmer and custodian of the Oklahoma County Courthouse. He quickly displayed a talent for real estate and newspaper work and dutifully wrote for Czech-language publications for nearly half a century. In 1912 he helped to establish the American Savings and Loan Association of Oklahoma City. He served as vice-president and treasurer of the firm until his

Karel D. Bicha

Matthew Anton Swatek. From the
Chronicles of Oklahoma. Courtesy
of the Western History Collections,
University of Oklahoma, and the
Chronicles of Oklahoma.

death in 1961. He founded the Oklahoma chapter of the Czech National Alliance, an organization created in the early days of World War I to promote the cause of national independence for the Czech lands, and played a prominent role in Czech-American fraternal societies. His activities won him a medal of honor from Thomas G. Masaryk, the first president of Czechoslovakia.[4]

Equally distinguished was the career of Matthew Anton Swatek of Oklahoma City. Born in 1867 in Prague, Swatek emigrated with his family in 1880 to Nebraska. A mason by trade, he nevertheless made the run of 1889 into the Unassigned Lands and homesteaded on Mustang Creek, southwest of Oklahoma City. In 1894 he entered the construction business, eventually organizing the M. A. Swatek Construction Company, a firm which he headed until retiring in 1935. His company built the first concrete road in Oklahoma, constructed many of the streets in Oklahoma City, Norman, Stillwater, and Perry, and erected the City Hall and Water Department Building of Oklahoma City. He served on the City Council and the Oklahoma County Excise Board. According to his son-in-law, "Mike" Swatek thought that fifteen hours was a normal working day.[5]

Most Oklahomans probably traveled unknowingly on Swatek's streets and roads. Others listened unknowingly to Bohumil Makovsky's

67

music. "Boh" Makovsky, born in 1878 in Frantisky, Bohemia, ended his career as head of the music department at Oklahoma Agricultural and Mechanical College and director of the college's concert band. He came to America in 1895, an accomplished violinist and clarinet player but with no educational credentials. He worked as a cigar maker and musician, and in 1903 he opened a music emporium in Oklahoma City. For many years he directed the bands at the Oklahoma State Fair. In 1916 he went to Stillwater to establish a music program at Oklahoma Agricultural and Mechanical College, an effort that ended with the creation of a distinguished concert band. He composed the school's marching music, and he helped to establish Kappa Kappa Psi, the national music fraternity.[6]

Most of these old settlers are no longer alive. But some of them took their time in departing. John Stolfa, born in the Moravian village of Tistin in 1866, turned up in 1893 in Ardmore and opened a tailor shop. In 1966 he still lived in Ardmore, and in nearly seventy-five years in Oklahoma had worked at four different occupations, reared twelve children, and collected the face value of his life insurance policy by outliving the predictions of the mortality table.[7] The old settlers were a hardy lot. Their passing signaled the end of much of the authentic Czech life in Oklahoma.

One aspect of Czech culture which declined with the passing of the old settlers was the common use of the Czech language. "It's gone," remarked a Bison, Oklahoma, housewife in 1978. "I think you'll find that with 90 percent of the families."[8] The disappearance of the language is hardly peculiar to the Czechs in Oklahoma. In all Czech-American communities the use of the language declined sharply between 1940 and 1960. A nationwide report on the prospects for "language maintenance" among ethnic groups in America concluded that the Czech language had a dim future.[9] But there is more to culture than language alone, and Czech Oklahomans have recently begun to rediscover other elements of their culture.

In the past decade a considerable revival of ethnic awareness has occurred in the United States. Automobiles which bear bumper stickers reading "Irish Power," "Italian Power," or "Kiss Me, I'm Polish" are only the external reflections of people suddenly conscious of their "roots." They have come belatedly to accept a truth pronounced long ago by the Jewish scholar, Horace Kallen: people may change their residences, their communities, their occupations, their religions, and their spouses. They cannot change their grandparents. Many, it seems, no longer want to.

Czech Oklahomans have begun to participate in the nationwide ethnic reawakening. Much of the current revival of Czech-consciousness in Oklahoma, however, represents the renewed ethnic consciousness of older people. Many of them are "second generation" Americans, the children of immigrants. In other parts of the United States the rediscovery of ethnicity is the work of the third and fourth generations in America. Nevertheless, in Oklahoma Czech Americans demonstrate their ethnic identity in two principal ways—Czech festivals and Czech days.

The two annual festivals held in Oklahoma are important events. The first festival occurred in 1951 in Prague, Lincoln County. Local promoters, searching for a unifying theme to use for a celebration of the fiftieth anniversary of the town's establishment, decided to utilize the Czech ancestry of many of the community's residents. Thus the *Kolache* Festival was born, an adaptation to community promotion of the commonest form of Czech pastry—*kolace* or "little cakes." Festivals occurred annually from 1951 through 1956, then lapsed until 1965. Since the latter year the festivals have occurred annually on the first Saturday of May, but commencing in 1979 the festivals will be held on the last Saturday of April. In recent years the festivals have attracted more than 20,000 persons. Except for *kolace, klobasy* ("sausage"), polka bands, and native costume, the festival is a typical middle-American community celebration.[10] Many of its features—the parade, the floats, the queen contest, the kangaroo jail, the street dance, the strolling troubadours—would be inconceivable in a Bohemian or Moravian village.

A second festival, the Czech Festival in Yukon, originated in 1966. Oklahoma Czechs, Inc., a private organization founded in that year, organized the first festival to commemorate the seventy-fifth anniversary of the founding of the Canadian County community. In 1969 the organizers of the festival prevailed upon Governor Henry Bellmon to designate Yukon as the "Czech Capital" of Oklahoma. Like the older event in Prague, Yukon's Czech Festival attracts more than 20,000 visitors and provides an opportunity for the reunion of friends and families.[11] Held annually on the first Saturday of October, the Yukon event offers the usual Czech foods, polka dancing, a parade, and a queen contest. One of the highlights of the event is the dancing of the *Beseda,* a blend of elements from sixteen Czech folk dances. The format of the festival varies little from year to year. "It's the tradition of the event that's important," explained the wife of the president of Oklahoma Czechs, Inc. "And it's kind of like a family

Children's *Beseda* group on "Kolache Day," 1973, Prague, Oklahoma. Courtesy of Mr. Roger Pritchett.

reunion."[12]

In more recent years "Czech Days" have been held in Hennessey and Bison. These are essentially parish activities sponsored by two Catholic churches with a large number of Czech parishioners, St. Joseph's in Hennessey and St. Joseph's in Bison. The format is simple and limited, consisting of a Czech-language mass, a dinner, and a dance. Czech Days began in 1976, and their frequency has increased in 1977 and 1978.

Czech Oklahomans involved in the promotion of Czech cultural activities in the state are optimistic about the future. Ethnicity is popular at the moment across the nation, but future interest in ethnic heritages is hardly guaranteed. Most of the Oklahomans who devote their time and energy to the preservation of Czech culture are persons of advanced years. Of the 230 members of Oklahoma Czechs, Inc., for example, nearly two-thirds are sixty-five or older. Ethnic consciousness obviously has not yet moved many in the younger generation to participate in cultural affairs. Nevertheless, there is at least one interesting project in a formative stage. In 1979 Oklahoma Czechs, Inc. will begin a language instruction program. This will be the first time Czech instruction has occurred in the state since the ZCBJ lodges abandoned their language schools in the 1930s. It is a hopeful sign—and a decent remembrance.[13]

Chapter 9
FOR FURTHER STUDY

Readers who wish to pursue the subject of the Czechs in America or the Czechs in Oklahoma beyond the confines of this booklet will confront some annoying obstacles. There is little writing about the Czech Americans available in English. Furthermore, much of the material is difficult to obtain. The original writings appeared in limited editions, and even large university libraries rarely have good collections. Public libraries have even less. Hence the suggestions for further study which are presented here are based upon the criterion of availability as much as quality, and the suggestions, for obvious reasons, are limited to English-language materials.

Anyone seriously interested in the subject of the Czechs in America must begin with the Czechs in their homeland. A brief, valuable, recent history of the Czechs is A. H. Herrmann, *A History of the Czechs* (London: Allen Lane, 1975). This book is available in the United States in a Penguin Books edition. A more detailed study of the Czech lands during the period of emigration to America is William V. Wallace, *Czechoslovakia* (London: Ernest Benn, Ltd., 1976). There are three rewarding studies which explore the general character of the peasantry—and nearly all of the Czech immigrants came from peasant backgrounds. Specifically useful is the book by Zdenek Salzmann and Vladimir Scheuffler, *Komarov: A Czech Farming Village* (New York: Holt, Rinehart and Winston, 1974). More general in character are Kenneth D. Miller, *Peasant Pioneers* (New York: Council of Women for Home Missions and Missionary Education, 1925; reprinted, San Francisco: R. and E. Research Associates, 1969), and Jerome Blum, *The European Peasantry from the Fifteenth to the Nineteenth Century* (Washington: American Historical Association Service Center for Teachers of History, Publication #33, 1960).

For the study of the Czechs in the United States, a timely and valuable bibliography has been published: Esther Jerabek, *Czechs and Slovaks in North America: A Bibliography* (New York: Czechoslovak Society of Arts and Sciences in America, 1976). This book is available from the Czechoslovak Society of Arts and Sciences in America, Editorial and Publication Committee, 225 Panorama Drive, Oxon Hill, Maryland 20021. The bibliography lists some 7,600 items, more than half of which pertain to the Czechs. Only a fraction of these items can be located with ease, and most of them are in the Czech language.

The basic works on the Czech-American experience, however, are easy to obtain. Though it is nearly sixty years old, the fundamental book is still Thomas Capek, *The Cechs (Bohemians) in America* (Boston and New York: Houghton-Mifflin, 1920; reprinted, New York: Arno Press and the *New York Times,* 1969). A useful supplementary source which contains a chronology and reproduces many documents is Vera Laska, *The Czechs in America, 1633–1977: A Chronology and Fact Book* (Dobbs Ferry, N.Y.: Oceana Publications, 1977). It is also worthwhile to read the sections on the Czechs in Emily G. Balch, *Our Slavic Fellow Citizens* (New York: Charities Publication Committee, 1910; reprinted, New York: Arno Press and the *New York Times,* 1969) and the colorful, opinionated interpretation of the Czechs in Edward Steiner, *On the Trail of the Immigrant* (New York: Fleming Revell, 1906).

There are some fundamental and easily obtained writings on the Czechs in the states of Nebraska, Kansas, and Texas, the states which contributed most of Oklahoma's Czech settlers. For general background consult the article by Frederick Luebke, "Ethnic Group Settlement on the Great Plains," *Western Historical Quarterly,* 8 (October, 1977): 405–430. Nebraska, the state of origin of most of Oklahoma's Czech pioneers, is the subject of the valuable compilation by Rose Rosicky, *History of the Czechs (Bohemians) in Nebraska* (Omaha: Czech Historical Society of Nebraska, 1929) and of Robert I. Kutak's unique volume, *The Story of a Bohemian-American Village* (Louisville, Ky: Standard Printing Company, 1933; reprinted, New York: Arno Press and the *New York Times,* 1970). Less important but still worthwhile are Francis J. Swehla, "Bohemians in Central Kansas," *Kansas State Historical Society Collections,* 13 (1913–1914): 469–501 and a book on the Texas Czechs, Estelle Hudson and Henry Maresh, *Czech Pioneers of the Southwest* (Dallas: Southwest Press, 1934).

A good place to begin the study of the Czechs in Oklahoma is the recent state history by H. Wayne Morgan and Anne Hodges Morgan, *Oklahoma* (New York: W. W. Norton Co., 1977). Land settlement in early Oklahoma is carefully examined in Solon J. Buck's old but useful "The Settlement of Oklahoma," *Transactions of the Wisconsin Academy of Sciences, Arts and Letters* 15, pt. 2 (1907): 325–79. The general subject of European immigrant groups in Oklahoma is treated in Douglas Hale's excellent article, "European Immigrants in Oklahoma: A Survey," *Chronicles of Oklahoma,* 53 (Summer, 1975): 179–203.

For Czech life in Oklahoma one item above all is mandatory: Russell Lynch, *Czech Farmers in Oklahoma; A Comparative Study of the Stability of a Czech Farm Group in Lincoln County, Oklahoma, and the Factors Relating to Its Stability,* Oklahoma Agricultural and Mechanical College *Bulletin,* vol. 39, no. 13 (Stillwater, 1942). Lynch also published his principal conclusions in an article, "Czech Farmers in Oklahoma," *Economic Geography,* 20 (January, 1944): 9–13. Lynch's studies dealt entirely with the Czechs of Lincoln County. Another work on the Lincoln County (Prague) area is Ronald Naramore, "Ethnicity on the American Frontier: A Study of Czechs in Oklahoma," *Papers in Anthropology,* 14 (Spring, 1973): 104–114. A brief survey of Czech settlement in other parts of Oklahoma is Hermina Rabstejnek, "A Tribute to Oklahoma and its Czech Pioneers," in Vlasta Vraz (ed.), *Panorama: A Historical Review of Czechs and Slovaks in the United States of America* (Cicero, Ill: Czechoslovak National Council of America, 1970), 58–62.

Some useful material may also be secured from county histories, community studies, and biographical sketches which appeared in magazines and journals. Foremost among these is Angie Debo's fascinating account of life in Marshall, Oklahoma: *Prairie City: The Story of an American Community* (New York: Knopf, 1944). Melva Losh Brown's *Czech-Town U.S.A.* (Norman: Hooper Printing Company, 1977), contains some valuable material on the Prague settlement. Prague is also the subject of two master's theses: Helen Herring, "A History of Lincoln County" (University of Oklahoma, 1943) and Roy A. Clifford, "A Social and Economic Survey of Prague, Oklahoma and Vicinity" (University of Oklahoma, 1947). Czech settlers figure prominently in Velma Musick (ed.), *Pioneers of Kingfisher County* (Kingfisher: Kingfisher County Historical Society, 1976) and less prominently in Guy P. Webb, *History of Grant County, Oklahoma, 1811 to 1870* (North Newton, Kansas: Grant County Historical Society, 1971).

There are also a number of interesting, brief biographies of

Czech Oklahomans. Donald Green told the story of Anton Caha in "Captain Caha's Mules," *Chronicles of Oklahoma,* 53 (Summer, 1975): 274-76. Florence Braun wrote an account of her father in "John Stolfa, Sr., From Tistin, Moravia, in 1866 to Ardmore, Oklahoma, in 1966," *Chronicles of Oklahoma,* 45 (Autumn, 1967): 307-11, and Luther Bohanon eulogized his father-in-law in "Matthew Anton Swatek," *Chronicles of Oklahoma,* 30 (Spring, 1952-1953): 134-35. The musician Bohumil Makovsky is the subject of an article by Geneva Holcomb, "Makovsky: The Man and the Musician," in *The A. and M. College Magazine* (September, 1930): 8–9, 19, and another article by Sam Whitlow, "Bohumil Makovsky, The Man," *The A. and M. College Magazine* (November, 1939), 6, 12. Rex Harlow contributed a biography of the Yukon flour miller John Kroutil in his book *Oklahoma Leaders* (Oklahoma City: Harlow, 1928), 354-63.

There are no specific writings on Czech society, religion or fraternalism in Oklahoma. Three articles by Robert L. Skrabanek on rural life among the Czechs of Texas contain information pertinent to Czech customs in Oklahoma, however. These are: "Forms of Cooperation and Mutual Aid in a Czech-American Rural Community," *Southwestern Social Science Quarterly,* 30 (December, 1949): 183-87; "Social Life in a Czech-American Rural Community," *Rural Sociology,* 15 (September, 1950): 221-31; and "The Influence of Cultural Backgrounds on Farming Practices in a Czech-American Rural Community," *Southwestern Social Science Quarterly,* 31 (September, 1951): 258-66. The Czech-American family is the subject of an excellent series of articles by Joseph Cada entitled "The Czech Family." These appeared, in English, in the Czech newspaper *Hlas Naroda ("Voice of the Nation")* from November 13, 1976 to January 1, 1977. (*Hlas Naroda* is a weekly publication of the Czech-American Heritage Center, 2657 South Lawndale Avenue, Chicago, Illinois 60623.)

On the complicated subject of religion, Joseph Cada's *Czech-American Catholics, 1850-1920* (Lisle, Ill: Center for Slav Culture, 1964) is a useful account. The freethinkers are the subject of only one published study in English: Karel D. Bicha, "Settling Accounts with an Old Adversary: The Decatholicization of Czech Immigrants in America," *Social History-Histoire Sociale,* no. 8 (November, 1972): 45-60. Though the style is difficult, it is also profitable to read Joseph J. Barton's essay, "Religion and Cultural Change in Czech Immigrant Communities," in Randall Miller and Thomas Marzik

Karel D. Bicha

(eds.), *Immigrants and Religion in Urban America* (Philadelphia: Temple University Press, 1977), 3–24.

There is little available writing on Czech-American fraternalism in Oklahoma. In the July, 1972 (vol. 75, no. 7) issue of *Fraternal Herald,* the official magazine of the Western Fraternal Life Association (ZCBJ), there appeared a history of the organization and of some of its member lodges, including Lodge Jan Zizka of Yukon and Lodge *Oklahomsky Rolnik* of Oklahoma City. *Fraternal Herald* is distributed to members of WFLA (ZCBJ), but it is rarely found in libraries. A convenient summary of the history and current state of the *Sokol* movement, however, is in Vlasta Vraz (ed.), *Panorama: A Historical Review of the Czechs and Slovaks in the United States of America,* 133–44.

Finally, it is a simple matter to secure information about the two annual Czech festivals held in Oklahoma. For details concerning the *Kolache* Festival contact the Prague Chamber of Commerce, Box 223, Prague, Oklahoma 74864. Comparable information pertaining to the Czech Festival in Yukon is available from Oklahoma Czechs, Inc., Box 211, Yukon, Oklahoma 73099.

NOTES

CHAPTER 1

1. Jan Kodes, quoted in Peter Bodo, "Why are the East Europeans Getting So Much Better?" *Tennis,* 13 (April, 1978): 60.

2. The reader who desires information about Czech history in addition to that offered in this survey should consult the following works: S. Harrison Thomson, *Czechoslovakia in European History* (Princeton, 1953); A. H. Herrmann, *A History of the Czechs* (London, 1975); William V. Wallace, *Czechoslovakia* (London, 1976); and Josef Korbel, *Twentieth Century Czechoslovakia* (New York, 1977). A good summary of eleven hundred years of Czech history also appears in the first chapter of John Gellner and John Smerek, *The Czechs and Slovaks in Canada* (Toronto, 1968).

3. Stanley Z. Pech, *The Czech Revolution of 1848* (Chapel Hill, 1969), p. 26.

CHAPTER 2

1. Wallace, *Czechoslovakia,* pp. 15–61.

2. Jerome Blum, "The Rise of Serfdom in Eastern Europe," *American Historical Review,* 62 (July, 1957): 807–36.

3. Emily Green Balch, *Our Slavic Fellow Citizens* (New York, 1910), pp. 75 *et passim.*

4. Johann Chmelar, "The Austrian Emigration 1900–1914," *Perspectives in American History,* 7 (1973): 337.

5. Kenneth D. Miller, *Peasant Pioneers* (New York, 1925), pp. 16–17.

6. Esther Jerabek (trans. and ed.), "Letters to Bohemia: A Czech Settler Writes from Owatonna, 1856–1858," *Minnesota History,* 43 (Winter, 1972): 141.

7. A convenient compilation of statistical data appears in Vera Laska, *The Czechs in America, 1633–1977* (New York, 1977), pp. 133–40. The best general study of the Czechs in the United States is Thomas Capek, *The Cechs (Bohemians) in America* (Boston, 1920).

8. Laska, *The Czechs in America,* pp. 1–63.

9. Karel D. Bicha, "The Czechs in Wisconsin History," *Wisconsin Magazine of History,* 53 (Spring, 1970): 194–204.

10. Laska, *The Czechs in America,* 61, 133.

CHAPTER 3

1. This verse is part of a larger poem called "The Captain's Mules." The author, Ezra Banks, was a litigant in the land claims cases which grew out of the run of 1889, and the poem dates from the early 1890s. The text of the poem appears in Dan Perry, "The First Two Years," *Chronicles of Oklahoma,* 7 (September, 1929): 286–88 and in Donald E. Green, "Captain Caha's Mules," *Chronicles of Oklahoma,* 53 (Summer, 1975): 274–76.

2. Solon J. Buck, "The Settlement of Oklahoma," *Transactions of the Wisconsin Academy of Sciences, Arts, and Letters,* 15 (1907): 325–79; H. Wayne Morgan and Anne Hodges Morgan, *Oklahoma* (New York, 1977).

3. Perry, "The First Two Years," 278–322.

4. Douglas Hale, "Anton Caha," unpublished manuscript, Oklahoma State University, n.d. The author is indebted to Professor Hale for providing a copy of this paper.

5. Undated memorandum of E. F. Best, U.S. Land Office Commissioner, in Bohemian Land Case Papers, Oklahoma Historical Society.

6. Hale, "Anton Caha," 1–2; Memorandum of William T. S. Curtis, U.S. Attorney for Oklahoma, March 17, 1894, Bohemian Land Case Papers.

7. Chase W. Mooney, *Localized History of Pottawatomie County, Oklahoma, to 1907* (Midwest City, Okla., 1971), p. 82.

8. *Portrait and Biographical Record of Oklahoma* (Chicago, 1901), p. 919. Caha's grave is in the Czech National Cemetery at Prague.

9. See Rose Rosicky, *A History of Czechs (Bohemians) in Nebraska* (Omaha, 1929); and Francis J. Swehla, "Bohemians in Central Kansas," *Kansas State Historical Collections,* 13 (1913–1914): 469–501.

10. Hermina Rabstejnek, "A Tribute to Oklahoma and Its Czech Pioneers," in Vlasta Vraz (ed.), *Panorama: A Historical Review of Czechs and Slovaks in the U.S.A.* (Cicero, Ill., 1970), 58–59; Charles E. Tigue, "The Czechs of Yukon," seminar paper, Oklahoma State University, 1974, 1–4; Velma Musick (ed.), *Pioneers of Kingfisher County 1889–1976* (Kingfisher, Okla., 1976), pp. 36, 45, 120–28, 136, 163.

11. Paula Jean Moyer, "Mishak, The Ghost Town," seminar paper, Oklahoma State University, 1974, 1–11, 15–17.

12. Helen B. Herring, "A History of Lincoln County," master's thesis, University of Oklahoma, 1943, 65–70; Ronald Naramore, "Ethnicity on the American Frontier: A Study of Czechs in Oklahoma," *Papers in Anthropology,* 14 (Spring, 1973): 104–5.

13. Rabstejnek, "A Tribute to Oklahoma and Its Czech Pioneers," 60; Guy P. Webb, *History of Grant County, Oklahoma, 1811 to 1970* (North Newton, Kansas, 1971), 124.

14. J. Hajek, "Cechove v Oklahome a jejich postup" (The Czechs in Oklahoma and their Development), *Amerikan; narodni kalendar na rok 1906* ("American; National Almanac for the year 1906"), 29 (1906): 227–32. *Amerikan,* an important source of information about the Czechs in America, was an annual publication (1878–1957) of the Chicago *Svornost* ("Harmony"), the first Czech daily newspaper in the United States.

15. Convenient compilations of population statistics pertaining to the Czechs in America appear in Capek, *The Cechs (Bohemians) in America,* pp. 59–62 and in Laska, *The Czechs in America 1633–1977,* pp. 133–36.

16. Douglas Hale, "European Immigrants in Oklahoma," *Chronicles of Oklahoma,* 53 (Summer, 1975): 179, 181, 195.

17. Josef Bunata, "Praha v Oklahome" ("Prague in Oklahoma"), *Amerikan; narodni kalendar na rok 1923* ("American; National Almanac for the Year 1923"), 44 (1923): 234–37.

CHAPTER 4

1. David Andelman, "Czech Catholic Church Struggles With Itself and the State," *New York Times,* February 27, 1978.

2. Karel D. Bicha, "Settling Accounts with an Old Adversary: The Decatholicization of Czech Immigrants in America," *Social History-Histoire Sociale,* no. 8 (November, 1972): 45–60.

3. Bruce Garver, "Czech–American Freethinkers on the Great Plains, 1871–1914," paper read at the Ethnicity on the Great Plains Symposium, University of Nebraska-Lincoln, April, 1978, 39pp.

4. Chicago *Svornost,* May 8, 1896.

5. Quoted in Alice G. Masaryk, "The Bohemians in Chicago," *The Charities,* 13 (December 3, 1904): 208.

6. Robert I. Kutak, *The Story of a Bohemian-American Village* (Louisville, Ky., 1933), pp. 41–51.

7. Garver, "Czech-American Freethinkers on the Great Plains, 1871–1914," 16.

8. Bicha, "Settling Accounts with an Old Adversary," 55–59.

9. Quoted in Garver, "Czech-American Freethinkers on the Great Plains, 1871–1914," 34.

10. Interviews with Frank Podest, Sr., November 18, 1978, Prague, Oklahoma; John Kouba, November 17, 1978, Yukon, Oklahoma; (Rev.) John Michalicka, November 15, 1978, Oklahoma City.

11. Thomas Elton Brown, *Bible Belt Catholicism: A History of the Roman Catholic Church in Oklahoma, 1905–1945* (New York, 1977), pp. 6–7.

12. (Rev.) Jerome Talloen, "Saint Joseph Church—Bison, Oklahoma: The Catholic story of a Czech settlement," manuscript in possession of the author; Yukon *Review,* October 8, 1978; interview with (Rev.) John Michalicka, November 15, 1978, Oklahoma City. Fire destroyed St. Martin's, Mishak, in 1953.

13. *Fifty Years for God and Country: St. Wenceslaus Parish, 1899–1949* (Prague, 1949).

CHAPTER 5

1. Angie Debo, *Prairie City: The Story of an American Community* (New York, 1944), p. 231.

2. See Capek, *The Cechs (Bohemians) in America,* pp. 164–221 for a thorough account of Czech-American journalism.

3. Tomas Capek, *Padesat let ceskeho tisku v Americe* ("Fifty Years of Czech Letters in America") (New York, 1911), pp. 81–85; Esther Jerabek, *Czechs and Slovaks in North America: A Bibliography* (New York, 1976), pp. 314–42.

4. The discussion of the Czech-language press in Oklahoma in the above para-

graphs derives from Capek, *Padesat let ceskeho tisku v Americe,* pp. 172, 173, 176, 177, 178, 192; Caroline Foreman, *Oklahoma Imprints, 1835–1907* (Norman, 1936), pp. 368, 391; Rosicky, *A History of Czechs (Bohemians) in Nebraska,* p. 390; and the N. W. Ayer and Sons, *American Newspaper and Periodical Directory* for the pertinent years 1905 through 1922. Peter Rabstejnek's autobiography appears in *Amerikan,* 69 (1946): 139–50; interview with Mrs. Peter Rabstejnek, November 15, 1978, Oklahoma City.

5. Alice Conner, "Fraternal Unions Show New Growth," *Milwaukee Journal,* May 3, 1978.

6. Josef Barton, "Religion and Cultural Change in Czech Immigrant Communities," in Randall Miller and Thomas Marzik (eds.), *Immigrants and Religion in Urban America* (Philadelphia, 1977), 9–15.

7. Josef Martinek, *Stoleti Jednoty CSA* ("A Century of the CSA") (Cicero, Ill., 1955), pp. 8–130.

8. The discussion of the development of ZCBJ in the above paragraphs is derived from "A Brief History of Our Association," *Fraternal Herald* ("Bratrsky Vestnik"), 75 (July, 1972).

9. Garver, "Czech American Freethinkers on the Great Plains, 1871–1914," 23–24.

10. Milly Krivanek, "Lodge Jan Zizka No. 67," *Fraternal Herald,* 75 (July, 1972), 26–28.

11. B. R. Karban to the author, May 23, 1978. Mr. Karban is secretary of Lodge *Vytrvalost* No. 217.

12. Lizzie Jezek to the author, June 28, 1978. Mrs. Jezek is secretary of Lodge *Oklahoma* No. 46. See also Russell W. Lynch, *Czech Farmers in Oklahoma: A Comparative Study of the Stability of a Czech Farm Group in Lincoln County, Oklahoma, and the Factors Relating to Its Stability,* Oklahoma A. and M. College *Bulletin,* vol. 39, no. 13 (Stillwater, 1942), pp. 94–100.

13. Tigue, "The Czechs of Yukon," 4–5; Naramore, "Ethnicity on the American Frontier: A Study of Czechs in Oklahoma," 110; (Rev.) John Michalicka to the author, March 2, 1978; Ed Genzer to the author, October 10, 1978, interview with Albert Vculek, November 19, 1978, Bison, Oklahoma.

14. A good introduction to *Sokol* is Walter Jerrold, "The Bohemian Sokol," *Fortnightly Review,* 94 (1913): 347–358; also valuable is Josef Cermak, *Dr. Miroslav Tyrs, Founder of the Gymnastic Organization Sokol* (Chicago, 1966).

15. "American Sokol Organization," in Vraz (ed.), *Panorama; A Historical Review of Czechs and Slovaks in the United States of America,* 133–44; *American Sokol,* 119 (February, 1978): 19.

16. Tigue, "The Czechs of Yukon," 3; Melva Losh Brown, *Czech-Town U.S.A.* (Norman, 1977), p. 137; Hajek "Cechove v Oklahome a Jejich Postup" ("Czechs in Oklahoma and their Progress"); 230; interview with John Kouba, November 16, 1978, Yukon, Oklahoma.

17. Brown, *Czech-Town U.S.A.,* 137; Mrs. Ellen Jeanne Schnabl to the author, April 5, 1978. Mrs. Schnabl is secretary of the American Sokol Organization.

18. "American Sokol Organization," in Vraz (ed.), *Panorama,* 133.

CHAPTER 6

1. Webb, *History of Grant County, Oklahoma, 1811–1970,* p. 211.

2. Interview transcript, Mrs. Frank Dvorak and Douglas Hale, June 8, 1975. The author is indebted to Professor Hale for providing a copy of the transcript.

3. *Our Alfalfa County Heritage* (Cherokee, Okla., 1976), pp. 312–13.

4. Lynch, *Czech Farmers in Oklahoma.* Much of the material in the remainder of this chapter is a summary of Lynch's findings.

5. Addison E. Sheldon, "Nebraska Czechs as I Have Known Them," in Rosicky, *A History of Czechs (Bohemians) in Nebraska,* 15.

6. Lynch, *Czech Farmers in Oklahoma,* p. 7.

7. Brown, *Czech-Town USA,* pp. 34–35.

8. A detailed explanation of the operation of beef clubs appears in Robert L. Skrabanek, "Social Organization and Change in a Czech-American Rural Community: A Sociological Study of Snook, Texas," Ph.D. diss., Louisiana State University, 1949, 259–60. Beef clubs also operated in Oklahoma.

9. Sheldon, "Nebraska Czechs As I Have Known Them," 15.

10. Roy A. Clifford, "A Social and Economic Survey of Prague, Oklahoma, and Vicinity," master's thesis, University of Oklahoma, 1947, 50–51; interview with Frank Podest, Sr., November 18, 1978, Prague, Oklahoma.

11. Bunata, "Praha v Oklahome," 234–37.

12. Rex Harlow, "John Kroutil," in *Oklahoma Leaders* (Oklahoma City, 1928), 354–63; interview with John Kouba, November 16, 1978, Yukon, Oklahoma.

CHAPTER 7

1. Bunata, "Praha v Oklahome," 234–37.

2. Zdenek Salzmann and Vladimir Scheuffler, *Komarov: A Czech Farming Village* (New York, 1974), pp. 98–101.

3. Skrabanek, "Social Organization and Change in a Czech-American Rural Community," 172–77; Robert W. Habenstein and Charles H. Mindel, "The American Ethnic Family: Protean and Adaptive," in Charles H. Mindel and Robert W. Habenstein (eds.), *Ethnic Families in America: Patterns and Variations* (New York, 1976), 415–19.

4. Jane E. Robbins, "The Bohemian Women in New York," *The Charities,* 13 (December 3, 1904), quoted in Laska, *The Czechs in America,* p. 113.

5. Edward Steiner, *On the Trail of the Immigrant* (New York, 1906), p. 193.

6. *Sooner Catholic,* January 8, 1978, 14–15.

7. Debo, *Prairie City,* p. 231.

8. Salzmann and Scheuffler, *Komarov,* 73; Glen L. Taggart, "Czechs of Wisconsin as a Culture Type," Ph.D. diss., University of Wisconsin, 1948; interview with (Rev.) John Michalicka, November 15, 1978, Oklahoma City.

9. Habenstein and Mindel, "The American Ethnic Family," 415. Interview with (Rev.) John Michalicka, November 15, 1978, Oklahoma City.

10. Steiner, *On the Trail Of The Immigrant,* 227–28, 235; Jane Addams, *Twenty Years at Hull House* (New York, 1910), p. 234.

11. Salzmann and Scheuffler, *Komarov,* p. 72; Steiner, *On The Trail Of The Immigrant,* p. 233.

12. Laska, *The Czechs in America,* p. 52.

13. (Rev.) John Michalicka to the author, March 2, 1978; interview with (Rev.) John Michalicka, November 15, 1978, Oklahoma City.